Róise Rua

PÁDRAIG UA CNÁIMHSÍ

Róise Rua

AN ISLAND MEMOIR

TRANSLATED BY

J.J. KEAVENY

MERCIER PRESS
IRISH PUBLISHER – IRISH STORY

MERCIER PRESS

Cork

www.mercierpress.ie

Trade enquiries to CMD,
55a Spruce Avenue, Stillorgan Industrial Park,
Blackrock, County Dublin

© Translation J.J. Keaveny, 2009

ISBN: 978 1 85635 624 4

10 9 8 7 6 5 4 3 2 1

A CIP record for this title is available from the British Library

This publication has received support from the Heritage Council under the 2009 Publications Grant Scheme

Mercier Press receives financial assistance from the Arts Council/An Chomhairle Ealaíon

Printed and bound in the EU.

CONTENTS

Introduction by J.J. Keaveny	9
Preface [1987] by Pádraig Ua Cnáimhsí	15
Foreword [1987] by Proinsias Ó Conluain	19
AUTOBIOGRAPHY	23
My Earliest Years	25
My Schooldays	36
My First Earnings	52
Working in the Lagan	64
The Knitting	82
The Life we had	91
Between Two Countries	98
Working at the Potatoes in Scotland	107
The Derry Boat	119
The Butcher	129
My Wedding Day	141
The Irishmen at Work in Scotland	148
Working at Home	159
Our Lives during the War	169
FOLKLORE	187
Peadar Breathnach in Arranmore	189
The Night of the Big Wind	196
The *Forest Monarch*	201

The Night of the Mollies   206

The Congested Districts Board   215

Dr William Smyth   223

The Lough Swilly Railway   229

The Whaling Station   235

The Year of the Yellow Grain   239

The Arranmore Drownings   245

RETROSPECT   253

Retrospect   255

My Life's Final Chapter   271

APPENDIX   280

INDEX   283

INTRODUCTION

It is, I feel, worth recording how one happens to spend a very considerable portion of one's life in an activity such as translation, and, specifically, how I came to devote so much of my time empathising with such a wonderful person as Róise Rua. A seminal moment was the day Raymond Gallagher handed me Pádraig's book in Spruce House, a respite centre under the aegis of Altnagelvin Hospital in Derry, Northern Ireland. 'You might find this interesting,' he said. 'It's in good, Donegal Gaeilge.'

Within days I was scanning the book and translating it simultaneously – the section on tattie-hoking – for the delectation of three fellow patients only to find that one of them had in fact worked in the potato fields of Scotland for ten years up to 1963. Another patient was very interested in Róise's adolescent years as a servant girl in the vicinity of his native Glenmornan in County Tyrone. He took the liberty of passing my translation of the 'Hiring Fair in Strabane' to the editor of *Concordia*, a local history magazine published in Strabane.

This prompted me to write to Pádraig Ua Cnáimhsí to explain/apologise for this unwarranted breach of copyright. Strangely, he was quietly pleased with the translation and welcomed the publicity it afforded the original. At this stage, however, copies of *Róise Rua* were sparse on the bookshelves – today they are virtually unobtainable and no wonder: there was just a single reprint and that in the year of the book's publication, 1988. Hopefully, this translation will generate an appetite for a long overdue reprint and further reprints; the authentic voice and experience of the impoverished people of West Donegal must not wither and die from neglect.

I fell in love with the book and after a little research composed 'Tattie-hokers' Weekend: July 1996'. Published in the *Derry Journal*, it was pinned up in the porch of the chapel in Arranmore by the late Fr Jimmy Shiels, who told me 'elderly men and women were moved to tears as they read it'. And this in turn led to my first meeting on Burtonport pier with Packie himself, and Anne Craig's broadcast of the poem on Radio Ulster from the chapel in June 1996. This was the first of many meetings with Packie, his wife Sheila and members of his family, and I well recall a conversation with Packie on the ferryboat, and his fervent wish that Róise's words, hopes and folklore should be passed on to the new millennium. As well as deepening my knowledge of times past, this work has greatly enlarged my circle of genuine, lovable friends.

When I was a little boy about to go to school in Moville, County Donegal, I noticed a clergyman frequently cycle past the house where I was born. Remarkably, he was talking to his dog – 'as Gaeilge', I was later told. This Church of Ireland rector was the Reverend Coslett Quinn, the scholar mentioned by Packie in his preface, and mentioned by Róise in the final chapter of the book. In his notes Coslett refers to conversations he had 'as Gaeilge' with the Galway-born manager of the Co-Operative Store. This man, my father, James A. Keaveny, had very good Gaeilge, and in one of his rare visits to his native Glenamaddy in Galway, he insisted that all the neighbours who gathered into the house should speak only Irish; the locals had come to see this local young man who'd done well for himself. This was the summer of 1933, and pockets of Gaeilge speakers were still to be found in the east of County Galway. My older brothers, aged ten, eight and six fell asleep to the susurrus of quiet conversation and slow airs on flute and fiddle – the sort of entertainment beloved of Róise throughout her life, and Ireland's staple fare throughout most of the nineteenth century and many centuries before that in spite of her mottled and troubled history.

I was privileged to share in one such night myself even though it was an American wake. Granted there was no dancing that night in O'Flaherty's house in Inishmaan, but there was the storytelling and the singing that Róise describes in her chapter on the Lough Swilly Railway, and, inevitably, there was the weeping and the keening down at the quay the following afternoon. That was in 1963, the year President Jack Kennedy came to Eyre Square. A Dublin teacher brought a television set to the school to enable the people of the island share in this new experience, but laudable as his intention was, I sensed a rudimentary tear in the Gaelic fabric that afternoon; the forest of hands raised by all those attesting to relatives in the US prefigured the rapid Americanising of our country.

Maybe I was mistaken, but that night in the same school three men sat in the darkness of the corner. The singer was in the middle; the man on his left took his right hand, the man on his right took his left hand and gently and slowly each drew the singer slightly to the right and then to the left in accord with the rhythm of the sean-nós song. A gentle sawing movement it was, unforgettable, iconic, and yet this performance evoked some ill-mannered sniggering from a few Dublin students blind to the ancient ritual being enacted in front of them. I was also privileged to have two hours on Inisheer while the *Naomh Eanna* was discharging and loading, currachs plying back and forth. Like Peadar Breathnach in the chapter bearing his name, I tore round that island gathering flowers from the fissures in the rocks and filling my pockets with wonderfully variegated little shells nestling in the very same fissures – almost in the manner Róise adopts as she combs a lifetime of experience and the many lifetimes adumbrated in her extensive 'library' of folklore.

Easter week 1952 saw our class spend wonderful days in the Gweedore Gaeltacht. Weeks studying *Cith is Dealán* exploded into reality in the bare, rugged landscape of Rannafast; language and terrain coalesced – the fabric was true. But First Arts Irish in UCD proved a stumbling block: Munster dialects and difficult seventeenth century texts saw me desert Gaeilge and specialise in English, philology being one of its many attractions. Preparing for the Ceard Teastas Gaeilge, the Irish language qualification for teaching at third level in the Republic, brought me back towards Gaeilge again. Reading through some discarded volumes of folklore in the library in St Columb's College, Derry saw me unconsciously moving in the direction my life and interests would take in the years of my quadriplegia. Missing from all this, however, was the daily conversation 'as Gaeilge'; it didn't affect me deeply at all, but a fellow patient in the National Rehabilitation Hospital in Dún Laoghaire, a Connemara man, was bereft of his language, and was profoundly grateful for my stumbling phrases and solecisms.

In Derry's Waterside Hospital student nurses from the Gaeltacht appeared from time to time. How glad I was when someone from, say, Annagary brought me my medicine. The talk flowed even if it was only reminiscences on my part of that week in the spring of 1952, the climbing of Errigal, the football match on an ebb-tide beach or the memorial to the victims of the tragic explosion on the shores of nearby Ballymanus nine years earlier – which crops up in the text. As does Paddy the Cope, who visited the Co-Op in Moville and its manager. My father never achieved anything as spectacular as landing the cargo of grain from the *Elfinoris*, though there were money-making opportunities a plenty in wartime Moville, packed as Lough Foyle then was with the fleets of the allies and their thousands and thousands of sailors.

Meanwhile I'm so glad to have spent such a long, lovely time in the company of Róise Rua and her gentle, ever-loyal devotee, Pádraig Ua Cnáimhsí.

J.J. Keaveny
Waterside Hospital
Derry 2008

PREFACE [1987]

Pádraig Ó Cnáimhsí

I am proud and blessed to have come across such a person as Róise in the course of my life, and to have had the privilege of writing her story. She possessed a wealth of Gaeilge folklore and song; she told me her story and I wrote it down. The hand-written pages lay at home a long time, and nothing was done about them. Eventually, when I retired from teaching in 1983, I set about arranging those pages and notes. I entered the manuscript in an Oireachtas competition in 1985 and it won the prize in its field. Publishers began to show interest, and this book is the fruit of my labour.

Caoimhín Ó Marcaigh is foremost among those who were especially helpful. He is my friend and next-door neighbour, and he saw to the publishing of the book; I can safely say the manuscript would still be lying around, page after page of it, unpublished, if he hadn't helped me. Caoimhín was the soul of generosity.

Dr Niall Ó Dónaill read the text and scrutinised the proofs; I'm extremely indebted to him; may he have a long and fruitful life.

Proinsias Ó Conluain, long a good friend of mine, has written the foreword; for that I am very grateful. No one in Ireland is better fitted to do that than Proinsias for he has spent his life working among the people in the Gaeltacht and in addition he's had some acquaintance with Róise herself: he spent a week in Arranmore talking to her when preparing a programme on her and her songs for Radio Éireann. As well as that, he visited the other islands of Donegal in his time here and gained a deep understanding of the islanders' way of life.

I extend my thanks very sincerely to Reverend Coslett Quinn for the help he gave me a long time ago. In his early years he collected a great amount of Donegal folklore, and when I mentioned I would like to read his collection, he warmly and generously allowed me do so.

Many, many others gave me assistance, but today I'm unable to name them all. Among them were many migrants who had spent their life working at home and abroad; my conversations with them deepened my understanding of the life our people led when working in Scotland. They greatly added to my knowledge on that topic, so it was much easier to write Róise's story after that.

It is patently obvious that the life Róise Rua and her contemporaries led is gone forever and a much more comfortable life is enjoyed by people today. The old world is gone and, just like the sluice that runs to the mill, that way of life will never come back again. If an account or description of those days is not written, people in the years ahead will have absolutely no idea of the way things were. Nothing will be left but echoes, and day by day those echoes will grow fainter and fainter. In any case, there's no need for us to spell out the like of that – it has been spelled out again and again for a long time past. It's what another islander – Tomás Ó Criomhthain – had in mind sixty years ago when he said: 'Do scríobhas go mionchruinn ar a lán dár gcúrsaí d'fhonn go mbeadh cuimhne i mball éigin orthu agus thugas iarracht ar mheoin na ndaoine a bhí im thimpeall a chur síos chun go mbeadh ár dtuairisc 'ár ndiaidh, mar ná bheidh ár leithéidí arís ann [I wrote a detailed description of events in our lives so that they'd be remembered to some extent, and I attempted to express in words the mindset of the people in my locality to ensure there'd be some record of us when we're gone, for there'll never be the likes of us again].'

Sources for photographs: *John McCauley, Meenmore, Dungloe who has since died, Peter McGee, Meenmore, Dungloe, Charlie Boyle (Dolly), Arranmore, Danny Boyle (Neilly Phil), Arranmore, Joe Boyle (Joe Phil), Arranmore and Burtonport who has since died, Phil Boyle (The Glen Hotel), Arranmore, Annie Boyle (Edward), Gortgar, Arranmore, Máire Ní Bhaoill, Peggy O'Boyle, Leabgarrow, Arranmore, The Scottish Tourist Board, Patsy McCormack, Alice Duggan, Kincasslagh, Pádraig Ó Dónaill, Patrick Dunleavy, Dungloe, Niall McGinley, Letterkenny, David Fleming, Antain MacGabhann, architect, Letterkenny who has since died, Patrick Carr, Alex MacMillan, Patrick Roarty, Sister Raphael, Gracie Rodgers, Iniskerragh and Dungloe, Nancy Rodgers (Maggie Bhúistéir) of Ploghogue and London, Doctor Peter Sweeney, Dungloe and Denis Tynan of Glenties.*

FOREWORD [1987]

Proinsias Ó Conluain

It was a fine sunny day early in May 1953 when I first met Róise Rua, the wife of Séamas MacGrianna, and that was the day I met Pádraig Ua Cnáimhsí for the first time too. Jimmy Mahon and I had just left Radio Éireann's outside broadcast unit in Burtonport, and we brought the most up to date tape-recorder with us into Arranmore. The great advantage of that recorder – the TR50 – was that it was portable; that's not to say, however, it was easy carried, but it was a great improvement on the old-fashioned system in vogue before then, the type that required records. The TR50 was ideally suited for the job in hand on this island in the Donegal Gaeltacht.

Seán Ó Súilleabháin of the Folklore Commission was a member of the Radio Éireann Council, and he's most likely the person who suggested we visit this amazing woman who had hundreds of songs. A sizeable portion of her folklore and songs had been written down the previous winter by Seán Ó hEochaidh, the Folklore Commission's man in Donegal. That's why Seán came along with us on our trip into Arranmore – he was very well informed on every aspect of life on the island; he was well known as a collector, and a seanchaí, a storyteller of note himself. We were only a couple of hours on the island when we met Pádraig Ua

Cnáimhsí, the head teacher in Aphort school, a man known for his knowledge of local history and everything pertaining to our Gaelic heritage.

After we'd had our tea the three of us – myself, Pádraig and Seán – walked east from Jack the Glen's Hotel to Screig an tSeabhaic, where Róise and her husband Séamas made us very welcome. Now that I've read Pádraig's book, I realise we were in the house that Séamas built after their wedding and by the cut of it few alterations had been made between then and the day of our visit. The house was very small, the roof and the door were low; there was an open fire in the kitchen, and there were two beds, one of which did service for want of chairs; he sat on the edge of the bed; a tall man in a mariner's cap, he didn't say much, just sat there listening to Róise talking and singing.

We didn't jot down a word from Róise that first day, but we arranged to meet her the following afternoon. She joined us in the hotel nearly every afternoon in the week we were there; in one of those sessions she sang us some twenty songs, not to mention the folklore associated with those songs, and the discussions she had with Seán over songs from Teelin and other areas.

Róise at that time was seventy-four, and there was nothing wrong with her voice or her memory. She was lively and young at heart, and at the same time had always a wry comment to make whatever the topic. Before she'd start singing she would drink a glass of gin neat – in one draught, no tonic, no mixer. After she had drunk another glass in the same fashion, she was now ready for work in earnest. We recorded around fifty songs, old songs in Irish and a big number of ballads in English. She had picked up the latter in the Lagan, in Scotland, or from

Arranmore people who had come back from America – songs such as *The Lily of the West, The Star of Philipstown, The Banks of Sweet Lough Rea, Murlough Shore, The Londonderry Lass* and lots of others that were popular in the nineteenth century. By the way, Pádraig's book ends where another book ought to begin – the story of Róise of the Songs – rather: Róise and the songs she sang. Perhaps Pádraig may address that topic; meanwhile, I'm pleased to hear that a cassette featuring some of her songs in the RTÉ archives is to be published by The Folk Music Society of Ireland. That cassette and Pádraig's book will give us a broad sweep of the qualities and gifts of this unique lady of song, who experienced many hard knocks but still made the most of life whenever a chance turned up, and at the same time gave pleasure to hundreds and hundreds by way of her songs.

Proinsias Ó Conluain

AUTOBIOGRAPHY

MY EARLIEST YEARS

I was born on 13 March 1879 in Sheskinarone about a mile from Dungloe in the Rosses of County Donegal. My poor mother, God be good to her, never had any book-learning during her life – in fact she couldn't even tell the time from the clock. In spite of that she had a handy way of reckoning my age: she used to tell me I came into the world around St Patrick's Day in the same year as the big priest, An Sagart Mór Ó Donaill, their parish priest, died. Hardship and poverty were widespread, and in my early years you heard the people mention the word *relief* again and again – *relief* roads, *relief* biscuits, *relief* clothes, and so on. It was very, very hard for people to stay alive in those days.

My father's name was Thomas Coll, and my mother's maiden name was Maighréad Ward. Because my mother's name was Maighréad, the people who knew me often called me Róise Mhaighréad, but I was also called Róise Rua because of my red hair. Later in life – after I became known as a singer – the Gaelic scholars were accustomed to refer to me as Róise na nAmhrán (Róise of the Songs). I'd answer readily to any of those names.

Although I may say I spent all my life on Arranmore, most of my relatives came from the mainland, and that applies to my husband too. And so we had relations on both sides of Arran

The house in Sheskinarone where Róise Rua was born.

Briny Sweeney's house in Acres early in the twentieth century. Róise's sister, Máire, spent a season there. The photograph was obviously taken in May – the potatoes have just been moulded, the haystack's now a lot smaller after the winter.

Roads. Seán Hiúdaí Ward from Belcruit was my grandfather on my mother's side. He married a woman named Máire from the Coll family on Cruit Island, but she died very young and he was left a widower early in his life. Some time after his wife's death, he took a trip into Arranmore to visit his relatives there, and while he was on the island he met my grandmother. A fondness developed between them; they pledged their troth to each other and married soon afterwards.

My grandmother's maiden name was Máire O'Donnell. She grew up in Ballintra, but married Manus Gallagher from Cloghcor and that's where they lived. Two years after they married Manus died in an accident when he and his brother Frank were fishing in Arran Roads. It was a holiday in the summer, and they went off in the currach in the afternoon to catch some pollock for their dinner. A swell probably struck them near Carrickvickeaghty. The currach overturned and they were pitched into the sea. According to the account we've heard, Frank managed to hang on to the gunwale until he was rescued; not so with poor Manus: he lost his grip and drowned.

He left behind him my grandmother and two children and, as we all know, people like her had no income of any kind in those days. It was totally different from the way things are today: no money was available to the likes of them – no dole, no pension, no school money, no security, nothing like that at all. No wonder widows were devastated when their husband died for often there was nothing to keep them from the poorhouse and ending their days there. Because of that, many widows tried to find another husband to ward off hunger and starvation from themselves and their children.

The long and the short of it was that the two widowed

persons, Seán Hiúdaí Ward and Máire O'Donnell, met each other and a match was made. As well as the two children she had by Manus Gallagher, Máire now had three daughters by her new husband Seán Ward: Róise and Bríd and Maighréad, my mother. Róise died while she was still only a child, and my mother was just fourteen when her own mother, Máire O'Donnell, died too.

My grandfather on my father's side was Donncha Rua Coll. He lived in Sheskinarone, and in his day he was very well known as a poitín-maker throughout the Rosses. Again and again the old people would tell of the day he swam across the river with the still on his back and a troop of revenue men in hot pursuit. The barracks at Meenmore was full of revenue men at that time, so it was extremely difficult for anybody to do anything unbeknownst to them. They were on the go day and night, constantly on the trail of poitín-makers. On this particular day it seems they came upon my grandfather stealthily while he was busy making a run of poitín. He was loath to lose his still, so there was no way out of it but to throw the still over his back and clear off. By the skin of his teeth he escaped their clutches, and somehow got himself and his still clear away from them.

Donncha Rua Coll had a large family, nine sons and five daughters. One of the sons – Thomas, my father – went to America early in his life and he spent a while doing all sorts of labouring out there – coal-mining in Pennsylvania, felling and sawing up trees, attending stonemasons building houses, jobs like that. After ten years or so out there he headed back home; he'd made up his mind not to return to America; he felt it would be far better to get married here and settle down at home. His bride was Maighréad, daughter of Seán Hiúdaí

The old revenue barracks at Meenmore. It was built at the end of the eighteenth century to house the redcoats in the Rosses. The revenue men were based there in Róise Rua's early years. It was burned to the ground in the War of Independence.

Ward from Cloghcor in Arranmore, but don't ask me how they met. My mother used to say they first came across each other at the fair in Dungloe, but their acquaintance deepened during my mother's visits to her relatives in Keadue. I'd say that's what happened; my mother was very friendly with her cousin, Bríd Bhriney Hiúdaí in Keadue and often went out to see her; it was a friendship that lasted throughout their life.

My mother and Thomas Coll had five children: Donncha, Kitty, Máire, Nuala and me. Donncha and Nuala died while they were still babies. Their deaths were caused by croup, a bronchial disease that was the death of many children back in those times. That disease is no longer widespread in this part of the country, thank God. Donncha and Nuala died while we were living in Sheskinarone; I've a notion my mother said Nuala was just a year old when she died.

My father was married only fourteen years when he died. He had injured his leg working in the forests in America sixteen years earlier, and the wound flared up again after he was back home. The leg began to worsen, and Doctor William Smyth – the dispensary doctor in the Rosses – couldn't cure the infection. He believed it was best to cut off the leg, but my father wouldn't hear of it. I remember my mother telling me what he said when the doctor suggested this: 'I'm going to the grave with the two legs God gave me.' He wasn't going to get any better at home, so the doctor decided to send him to the hospital in Glenties.

At that time there was a small hospital in Glenties; it's closed now for it was no longer needed once they opened the new hospital in Dungloe. My father went to the small hospital; it had been there from the time the poorhouse was built during the Famine. At that time the roads in this part of the country were desperate, and it was a very long distance you had to travel before you arrived at Glenties. A neighbour of ours – Tarlach O'Donnell or Tarlach Mhánuis – helped him make the journey that day. They brought a horse and cart to the house, and Tarlach and the man who owned the horse carried out my poor father and laid him in the well of the cart. They had put an old chaff-filled mattress in it and my mother wrapped a couple of quilts around him to keep him warm on the journey.

Even though I was barely four at the time, I still remember that day. I started to cry when the cart went down the road and my mother had to take me inside. Little did we think that day that my father was never to come back to us again.

My mother told me afterwards she tried her best to visit him once a fortnight, even though it would be far from easy

The old hospital in Glenties, It was opened as a Poor House and also as a hospital in 1846. After 1923 it no longer functioned as a Poor House but remained in use as a hospital until 1958 when a new hospital was opened in Dungloe. The old building was demolished, and in 1968 a Community School was opened on the site. In April 1883 Róise Rua's father died in the old Glenties hospital.

for her. She had to make that long journey to Glenties and back on foot – poor people had no other means of transport then. Occasionally she might go by Doochary, but most of the time she and the other women went by way of Ballinacarrick. They'd go straight on from Dungloe, through Derrydruel and on as far as Cloghwally; then they'd take the shortcut up to Ballinacarrick. They would cross the Gweebarra River by the tidal ford, and walk on through Derryloaghan to Shallogans, and from there on down to Glenties. They were able to cross the causeway at low tide or even at half tide, but if the tide was fully in, they had to hire a boat to take them across at

Ballinacarrick. It cost sixpence to go across, but whenever there were as many as six on the boat, they only had to pay a penny. You can be sure my mother was seldom on her own, for lots of women made that journey up to Glenties and back again, every one of them with a small bundle of thread or stockings on their back. You can be sure my mother too did the same as the others, for she was determined to earn whatever she could from the knitting. We were children at that stage; every penny she could get was sorely needed.

My father was just half a year in Glenties when he died. As well as the illness he already had, he was struck down by the flu or some other winter ailment, as far as I know. He was buried up there. Later on, when I began to understand things, I asked my mother why his remains weren't brought home; she did her best to give me an answer. The snow, she said, lasted eight weeks that year; the weather was so severe a cart couldn't get as far as Glenties; instead of being brought down to be buried at home my father's corpse had to be buried in the graveyard up there.

Life was hard for people then, and it was particularly rough on us during my father's long illness, for my mother had no money coming in apart from the odd shilling she'd earn from knitting the queen's stockings for the 'gentleman in Glenties'. She had debts too, and to clear them and pay the rent and rates she had to sell some of my father's land to our neighbour, Tarlach O'Donnell. It was Tarlach too who bought the rest of the land when my mother remarried shortly before moving into Arranmore. 1883 was the year my father died, God rest him, and my mother used to tell us he was about sixty when God called him. Two years later my mother married the Búistéir, and soon after that we all came in here to live in the island.

Within a year of my father's death a man from down the country proposed to my mother, but she turned him down; she felt it was no great burden on her to stay single a couple of years at least out of respect for the good man she had lost.

Two years after my father died, my mother visited relatives of hers in Arranmore, and it was during that visit that something happened that proved to be a turning point in all our lives. A friendship developed between her and a man from the island, Antain Gallagher, an affection and a companionship that was to remain unbroken from then on. In a short time a match was made between herself and Gallagher. They were married soon afterwards and the matter ended with her selling the place on the mainland and going to live with her new husband on the island. She took Kitty, Máire and me with her; on account of that I was reared in Arranmore, and it's here I have lived ever since. Antain Gallagher was the name of our step-father; however, the people of the island seldom called him by his first name or his family name; because he practised butchering in his youth he was never called anything except 'the Búistéir'.

I was about six years old when I came to the island. Máire my sister was about nine, and Kitty, the biggest, was eleven or so. I still remember clearly the first day we came into the island with Patrick ('the Laddie') Boyle; he had come out for a cargo of potatoes. I remember us sitting in the boat at the quay in Burtonport, looking at the men loading bags of potatoes on the boat. We knew absolutely nothing about the sea at that time as we sat there leaning out over the gunwale, staring down into the water. We landed at Trá Ishkirt, and had a long walk ahead of us to our new house, for it was situated up at the head of the slope on the way out to the lighthouse. The Búistéir himself, the man of the house, came out to meet us;

Burtonport Harbour as it was in the early years of the twentieth century. Shortly before this the quay was lengthened. In 1903, Burtonport was connected by rail to Letterkenny.

he gave us a great welcome, and he led us inside. We were cold from sitting in the boat at the quay before crossing into the island, but we didn't stay cold for long for he'd a fire blazing for us – a fire that would roast a sheep! We were all of us delighted to be there at long last.

Since I was only six, I remember very little of the years before I came into Arranmore. Even though my sisters – Kitty and Máire – attended school on the mainland, I didn't go until I came to the island, and that's probably why I didn't know many other children in the area. Kitty and Máire attended Meenmore School, but my mother decided I wasn't old enough yet. The school was about a mile away and it wouldn't be easy for the likes of me to walk that distance. There was another reason too: my mother wouldn't be able to send me to school unless she had warm clothes for me and a new pair of boots as well; as things were, she probably felt she had more than enough in hand making sure there were clothes and boots for Kitty and Máire; she was in no hurry to send me to school.

MY SCHOOLDAYS

There were two schools on the island in my young days, the same as there are today: Leabgarrow School and Aphort School. John Stoupe Charley, the new landlord, founded both schools shortly after he came to the island; that was shortly after the year of the Famine. He set up a school in Iniskerragh as well. The Búistéir – God be good to him – lived a long life and had an exceptional memory; he used tell us that the priest and the people helped the landlord build those schools. Not only was Mr Charley the founder – he was the manager of these schools as long as he had control over the island. During my actual schooldays therefore and during the winters when I went to school afterwards, the priest of the island wasn't in charge of the school – the running of it stayed in the hands of the landlord and his agents, Hugh Montgomery, George Magee and so on.

Máire and I were sent to school soon after we arrived in the island. Máire was a couple of years older, and I still remember her taking me by the hand every morning as we left the house on our way to school. We had to walk about a mile every morning and we had a bare, open road ahead of us with no shelter whatsoever. We had no trouble going down to school in the morning: we had the slope with us, and most of the time the wind was with us as well. But going home

Schoolchildren at Leabgarrow on the day the school opened in 1908.

was often a very different story. There was a steep slope to climb and often – especially during the winter – gales raged from the north and we had the full blast of it straight in our faces. And there were many times too when the children had to stand outside the school in the morning, waiting for the master to come and open the door. It wasn't that he was late; no, it happened because the pupils arrived too early. There were only two watches on the island at that time and there was hardly a house with a clock. So there were days when the pupils turned up too early and had to shelter at the gable until the master came.

Our school wasn't very big; in fact there was just the one room, and that was enough for we had only one teacher. You couldn't say it was a tall building, and I feel it was built low deliberately for it stood on as bare and exposed a spot as you'd get on the west coast of the country; because it was built that way the wind wouldn't be too strong for it. It had a felt roof and as far as I could see it was sound enough for there were

The Glen House Hotel today. The Glen House was built by John Stoupe Charley when he became landlord of the island. He lived in it from 1855.

no leaks in it. But there was one drawback to the felt: it made the room hotter on a warm summer's day; it wasn't often we had that kind of weather; we seldom had 'a day to make the lint blow'. At the same time we had more space then for there weren't as many children at school then; many children, especially those who were really badly off, were away working – making kelp, saving the turf, hired out in the Lagan, and so on.

My school stood on the place they still call the Páirc na Scoile (The School Field); it was knocked down a long time ago; the ballog (wallsteads) and everything else are all gone. It was situated on a hill about three hundred feet above sea level, so there was always a great view from it on a nice summer's day. From the gable, we had no trouble seeing Tory Island, Bloody Foreland, Errigal, Muckish, Sliabh Sneachta and all the hills of Donegal.

John Stoupe Charley (1828–1878) purchased the Arranmore estate from Landlord Conyngham in 1849, and took up residence on the island. He died in Dún Laoghaire, County Dublin.

A new school was built here in 1908 near the shore at Leabgarrow, and the old one up at the Páirc na Scoile in Gortgar was no longer needed; like Tara of old it was abandoned.

Daniel Boyle was our master; we were lucky to have such a nice teacher. He always did his best for us and was never sore on us; he'd often threaten us, but rarely slapped anyone. He taught us entirely through English, yes, even our religious knowledge too! He'd warn us not to be talking in Irish, but we paid little heed to that for we found it difficult to speak English – we weren't at ease in that language. Irish was the language we had from our childhood and it was the language of our everyday speech. If the master addressed us in school, we had to make a really hard effort to answer in English; apart from that most of us spoke nothing but Irish; it was the language of our nightly chats round the fire; we spoke it on our way to school and on our way home again; we spoke it in the shop; it was the same when we went to confession, and so on. But there were pupils in the school who hadn't a word of Irish: the children of the lighthouse-keepers, the policemen, the coastguards; in the school too were the children of the men who worked for the landlord – the agent, the steward, the people who looked after his cattle, and so on; English is what every one of them spoke.

I still remember the books I had at school. There wasn't much in the First Book (the Red Book) apart from the alphabet; it only cost us a halfpenny. Then we went on to the Second Book (the Green Book) and paid a penny for it. Often the pupils with these books sat on stools along the walls while the older pupils worked at the desks. It wasn't easy for the teacher in a school like that to give us all a good education, for there were times when he'd have too many pupils and often there wasn't a trained person to give him a helping hand. He'd often ask one of the bigger pupils to assist him in some way; for instance, he could give out spellings to the weaker pupils.

Master Boyle told us lots of lovely stories – some of them out of the Bible, others from books he read to us – and I'd always listen very attentively. He didn't neglect poetry either, and made us learn, word for word, the poems in our books. Poetry or recitation was something I loved and to this very day I can quote some of those poems I learned long ago. I liked a song by the name of *Erin go Bragh* and another entitled *The Blind Man*:

> Slowly down the village street
> with his dog and with his staff,
> listening to your passing feet,
> listening to your merry laugh,
> looking with a vacant eye
> in your face he cannot scan,
> telling all that passes by
> goes the poor blind man.

I managed to stay at school until I was in Fifth Book, so I had a smattering of learning for the rest of my life. You have to realise there were many children of my age at that time who had absolutely no learning at all. That made life very difficult for them and others like them when they went to work in the Lagan or across in Scotland later on, for they weren't able to write a note home to their family and had to rely on someone else to do it for them. Thanks be to God, that problem didn't arise in my case; I was always able to manage for myself.

As I've said already, Máire and I went to school together; Kitty, our oldest sister, wasn't with us: she had to be hired out to earn a few pennies to help my mother bring us up.

Arranmore Lighthouse. It was built in 1798 at the request of Colonel Burton Conyngham, then landlord of the Rosses and the island. Grattan's Parliament had spent more than £40,000 establishing a fisheries station in Rutland Harbour, and the landlord argued that a lighthouse would be of benefit fishermen and sailors.

Money was scarce and it wasn't easy for fathers and mothers to dress their children for school. Our step-father, the Búistéir – the man God put in charge of our family – was a good breadwinner; as for my mother she was as able a housewife as you'd find anywhere in the three parishes. I remember she used dress us for school in tweed with a lining of fine white homespun underneath. And now that I'm talking about clothes, my mother had her own spinning wheel and that was a great help to us all. Every year she spun the sheep's wool, and spinning and knitting for us kept her busy throughout the winter.

My mother bought me a pair of boots for my first communion, but I didn't wear them very much, but minded them as carefully as the eyes in my head. To the best of my memory, she paid just four shillings and sixpence for them. I was always saving them for fear of dirtying them or damaging them in any way, and most of the time I'd walk to school in my bare feet. I never stopped polishing them by the fire at night for they were the first pair of shoes I ever had – no wonder I was dying of pride about them. Indeed one snowy day my mother came to the school to carry me home on her back sooner than let me trudge barefoot in the snow. At last she told me to throw my first communion boots away: they were getting too small for me; it'd be better to give them to a child they would fit – sure, wasn't I the last child in the family!

At that time the children from Arranmore lighthouse attended school along with us. There were upwards of eight children there – the Higginbottoms and the Williamses. Since they had to walk three miles to school every morning, the Williams children had a donkey for the journey. The poor donkey could carry no more than two at a time, so they took turns on her, a pair now, and then another pair. I remember them well – John, James, Henry and Sarah. Sarah and I were the same age, and travelling the same road to school every day and home again we were really close friends and often she'd let me ride with her on the donkey. That donkey was the placid animal, easy to handle with the halter.

The lighthouse children were Protestants and every afternoon they were allowed home before us. The master always taught religion at half-past two, and that's when the Protestant children left. There was a chart on the wall; on one side it read *Secular Instruction*, and *Religious Instruction* on the other. At half-past two Master Boyle would turn round the chart to *Religious Instruction* and the Protestant children would head away for the lighthouse.

There were no free lunches in our days as there are today. My mother made two school-bags for Máire and me. She made a belt for fastening the school-bags and we were able to carry our bags over our shoulder to school and back. My mother gave us each a piece of bread and butter in the morning if she had done some baking, but there were many, many days we had no lunch at all and we were starving with hunger by the time we got home in the afternoon. The Búistéir always had a good warm fire for us, and my mother was sure to have a big pot of poundies ready for our dinner; poundies was what we had most of the time.

For six weeks or so we had the good fortune to get free biscuits at school. It was always in the depths of winter – in January – that the biscuits were divided among us; I believe it was a charity or a committee in Dublin that paid for them. We were the happy children at lunchtime every day when the master gave us our share of the biscuits.

George Magee, the landlord's agent, had two children – Joe and Jane. When I first knew him, he was working for John Stoupe Charley, and was living in Leabgarrow, in the house where the Ward family are today. He had the post office then and a shop; his shop was the first in the island. Not many letters were sent or received at that time, and if it happened there was a letter for somebody, Magee sent word to him and he was obliged to come for it himself – there wasn't the delivery service we have today. When the person received his letter, he had to pay a fee of sixpence. This Magee I'm talking about hadn't a scrap of Irish; worse still, he was as deaf as an axe. During his time as agent and manager of the schools in Arranmore and Iniskerragh, it was his custom to give the schoolchildren a picnic every year; I'd say he was continuing a custom landlord

A group of people on Leabgarrow Strand at the beginning of the century. Leabgarrow School was built in 1908; this photograph evidently was taken sometime before that. From the left: Jack Boyle (Néill Johndy) Leabgarrow; two boys, Jack Byrne, Leabgarrow, the other boy's name we do not know; two ladies on holiday; Sheila Boyle (Síle Bhig John Neansaí), Leabgarrow; her husband, Charlie Boyle (Liam); Phil (Mór) Boyle (John Neansaí), Scraigathoke; a visitor; Phil Boyle (Néill Neansaí), Leabgarrow, and another visitor. All the visitors were staying in the Glen House.

Charley had started. In his day when the landlord administered the schools personally, he gave the children a picnic once a year on the lawn in front of 'The Big House'. He died a year before I came into the world, but the custom was carried on. Every year we looked forward to the day of the picnic and no wonder, for the only picnic the schoolchildren ever got back in those times was the one Magee gave them. Would you believe it – all through my life ever since my days at school I've never been to another picnic!

I was nine years old when I first left school to be hired. The hiring always took place in the summer and after that I'd go back to school for the winter. Later when I came back from my hiring time in the Lagan, Master Boyle was gone; the new teacher, Master Carr, came from Fanad and he stayed a long time on the island; in fact he stayed till he went out on the pension. He had good Irish, so everyone found him easy to talk to. He came to our house one day and advised my mother to send her two girls, Máire and me, to the school for the winter. I didn't mind in the slightest but Máire was now a grown girl and she felt a bit uneasy about it. I still remember what the master said to her: 'Don't be a bit embarrassed, girl. You're wiser now, and a winter at school will do you the world of good. You'll learn as much in two months now as you'd learn in a whole year back then.'

We took his advice and went back. Years later the truth of the old saying came home to us: 'Learning is easy carried, but the lack of it is a heavy burden.'

Father Anthony Gallagher was stationed on the island when I made my first communion. Máire and I made our first communion on the same day. I recall clearly the day the priest came to the school to talk to us; he gave us a short examination to find out if we clearly understood what the sacraments were. Goodness me, the questions he asked weren't a bit difficult. And I remember too the clothes I got for the big day: the skirt was blue, the coat was plaid and belted, and I had a bright ribbon. Máire was dressed in exactly the same style. My mother bought the makings of a blouse for each of us – a linen blouse to match the plaid coat. Everybody that met us said we were a credit to her.

We did our writing on slates at that time. We used them in school during the day and took them home as well. A pen cost only a halfpenny, but we got six sticks of chalk for a penny, and that's what we used for writing on the slates.

As long as we were at school we were seldom absent unless there was a good reason for staying home. My poor mother had absolutely no learning; she was determined we'd not go through life as she had. She knew the day would soon come when we we'd have to leave school and work for a living; so she tried to ensure we attended school regularly as long as we were pupils. It was unusual for us to be absent more than one or two days in the year.

The Búistéir told us Master Boyle came to the island when the teacher before him – Master Patrick O'Donnell – was sacked. This O'Donnell was said to have links with the *Molly Maguires*; not only did he serve time in prison, he lost his job as well. The new master was a Dungloe man; the Boyles were capable, talented people; one of his brothers was a lawyer across in England and it was said he had two sons in the Redemptorists.

Master Boyle's wife was Bríd Daly from Gartan and they had a family of four – Máire, Nora, Bríd and Condy. Condy taught in the school now and again in the last years when ever the master wasn't well. Condy's own health soon took a turn for the worse, and he didn't live long after that. He died in 1893 and was buried in the new graveyard that was opened in the island that year; in fact he was the first person to be buried there.

Máire Boyle married Seán Ward, Seán Taig. I got to know him really well, for he was a gaffer in Scotland; my sister, Máire, and myself were tattie-hokers in his squad all our years at the potatoes. Nora Boyle married Master Huidie Rua O'Donnell of Ploghogue on the west side of the island; he had a shop and

Arranmore teachers in 1941: Packie Boner, Charlie Boyle, Mickey Boyle and Barney Gallager, seated.

a pub. Master Boyle's other daughter, Bríd, married one of the Ward clan in Aphort; they went off to America.

There was never a schoolmaster's house in Arranmore, and the teachers often found it difficult to get lodgings. Master Boyle couldn't get a house to rent after he came to the island

and himself and his family had to live in part of the schoolhouse. That wasn't a satisfactory situation at all, so he decided to leave Arranmore. When the landlord got to hear of this, he gave the teacher a house and farm to persuade him to stay. At this stage Hugh Montgomery had left the island and George Magee was the new agent. Charley Beag, the landlord, set Magee up in a new house and farm in Leabgarrow, and gave the agent's house in Fallagowan to Master Boyle. That's where he was living when I got to know him; his people live there still.

Life has changed greatly over the past three score and seven years; the life we had then was much, much tougher than the life youngsters have today; they have a far more enjoyable time, they have far more comfort. You may come across people who'll say money is still very scarce, but I can assure them there's lots more money around now than there was when we were children. The only money they got then were the few pennies they toiled for at the fishing, or the wages they earned in Scotland, or the Lagan or across in America. They had no other source of money; huge numbers were absolutely down and out; it was well nigh impossible to rear a large family on next to no money, most of them lived hand-to-mouth.

People's houses are better, food is better, clothes and foot-wear are better, and in general, children are a thousand times better off in every way; on top of that they don't have to do a scrap of work the whole year round. In former times there was no end of jobs for schoolchildren: herding the cattle, drawing loads with the donkey in the spring, milking the cows, bedding them, working at the hay or corn in autumn, gathering potatoes and so on – there was no let-up from one end of the year to the other. Tillage isn't done the way it was done long ago, so there's none of that sort of work for children any more. They stay at school until the law allows them to leave, and after they leave school on the island many go on to college for more education.

In today's world the children no sooner out of the cradle than they're wearing watches! In my childhood the only people who had watches were the priest, the schoolmaster, a policeman and the men who manned the lighthouses. There was no clock in the school, so we had no idea of the time. The master of course had a watch, and he'd take it out of his pocket twenty times a day to see the time. In summer it was easy to tell the time from the shadows the sun cast through the windows or on the side of the door, but that wasn't possible on a dark winter's day, so we had to wait patiently till Master Boyle told us it was time up; we were the happy ones when he announced that the Protestant children could now go home. He'd recite *The Angelus* and then move on to Religious Instruction.

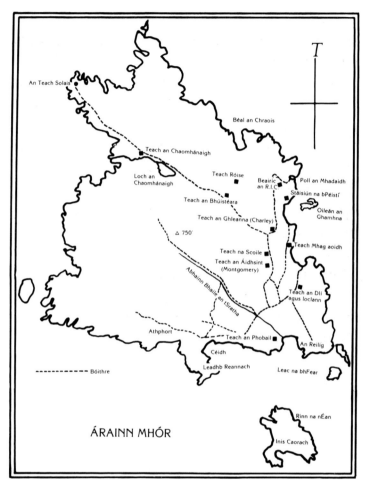

From the top:
An Teach Solais – the Lighthouse; Teach, Loch an Chaomhánaigh –
Cowan's Lake; Teach an Bhúistéara – the Búistéir's House; Róise Rua's
House; RIC Barracks; Poll an Mhadaidh – Pollawaddy;
Stáisiún na bPéistí – the Whaling Station; Oileán an Ghamhna
– Calf Island; Charley – The Glen House; Teach Mhag aoidh – Magee's
house, Leabgarrow; Teach na Scoile – School, built 1908; Teach an
Áidhsint – Agent Hugh Montgomery's house; Teach an Dlí agus íoclann
– Courthouse and Surgery; Teach an Phobail – Chapel; An Reilig – the
Graveyard; Ceidh – Aphort Pier; Inis Caorach – Iniskerragh; Rinn na
nÉan – Rinnanean; Abhainn Bhaile an tSratha – Ballintra River.

MY FIRST EARNINGS

As I mentioned already I was just nine years old the first time I left school to be hired. Soon after the feast of St Brigid, 1 February, the soil had to be tilled and children were hired out to people busy at their spring tasks. There were jobs of all sorts to be done inside and outside the house, and boys or girls were taken on to help at the washing and cooking, milking the cows, cleaning out the byres, feeding the cattle, cutting and setting seed potatoes, keeping an eye on the children, and so on. Our Máire was hired out to Paddy Brian's in Inishfree Upper, but I hadn't to go as far away as that. Cousins of ours, the Gallaghers of Illion, needed a servant girl, so my mother sent me to work for them. I went after St Brigid's Day and was away until the end of April. It was my first time away from home, and it was all very new to me. I was often homesick during the first few days, but I was kept so busy that the work got the better of me and I hadn't much time to be thinking of home; by bedtime I was so tired that as soon as my head touched the pillow I fell fast asleep. It wasn't that the work was heavy – I just didn't have a lot of strength then.

Potatoes were only eighteen pence a peck at that time, and – would you believe it – even though I was only three months away from home, I had the price of a barrel of potatoes home with me at the beginning of May! My mother was proud of me and she was delighted when I handed her the fifteen shillings – the pay I got from the man in Illion. I was happy too, to be back home again after my first spell of hiring.

I was next hired out in Iniskerragh; I spent three seasons there before I went to the Lagan. Iniskerragh is a small flat island in Boylagh Bay a mile or so south of Arranmore; the highest spot is no more than fifteen feet above sea level. It contained some fifty acres of land – soil as fertile as you'd find on any island round the coast. From away back in the past, the people depended on fishing and migration for their livelihood. In the last century they earned a lot of money harvesting kelp, but for the last forty years there's been no money in it. There were eleven tenants on the island when I was there, between seventy and eighty people lived there. Iniskerragh was abandoned in 1955; some of them went to Arranmore, others settled on the mainland; it's deserted now.

In some ways life on Iniskerragh was different from our life back in Arranmore. There was a school but there was no priest or chapel, so to attend mass on Sundays the islanders had to go to Arranmore. That was easy enough in the fine weather in summer, but there were Sundays in winter when crossing over was impossible. When that happened, they'd all gather up in the school or in one of the houses and recite the fifteen decades of the rosary. Twice a year they had the Stations on the island – in Lent, and again in October.

Many of the teachers on Iniskerragh long ago had never seen the sea until then. They usually didn't stay very long, most of them leaving after a year or two. In my first year the teacher was a young man by the name of John Longhorn; he came from somewhere up the country. He was gone, however, when I went across the following year. I got to know him well, for

The row of houses on Iniskerragh Island long ago. It's autumn; the turf has been brought in from the mainland and stacked close to the houses. The walls are a rampart against the sea.

he lodged in the house I was hired in. He wasn't much more than twenty, and as far as I could make out he had taught nowhere else before coming to Iniskerragh. He was a nice, pleasant, good-natured man, and lively and generous. When he left, another young man from Meendrain, Dungloe arrived and he spent about a year there. After that he got a teaching post on the mainland and spent the rest of his life out there. That was John Doherty, and when he left, his brother Michael took his place. The two of them are dead now, God rest them. Michael became an inspector and passed away in Dublin a few years ago; he had some fame as a writer; a couple of books were published containing folklore he had collected.

The school in Iniskerragh was very small – just one room in a dwelling house the landlord had reserved from a tenant long ago; it was part of Phil Rodgers' house, and that room, as I

Phil Rodgers's house on Iniskerragh Island. There was just a single well on the island so water was often scarce in summer. Spoutings and barrels were in constant use for collecting rainwater.

said, served as a school for the people of the island. It probably wasn't really suitable, for it was situated right in the middle of the row of houses. A new school was built at Rinnanean many years later; it stood some distance from the line of the other houses.

For my first two years I worked for Danny Den O'Donnell and his wife Isobel; a nicer couple you wouldn't find if you were to walk the country from one end to the other. They were just lovely. They treated me as one of their own especially where food was concerned, and they were always warm and generous to me. No wonder I went back the second year as soon as they sent word to me. My pay for each of the two half-years was two pounds ten shillings. I'd go across after St

Patrick's Day and stay there till the beginning of November. Out on the mainland the hired children were kept working up to 12 November, Old Samhain, but in Iniskerragh they always paid me at Hallowe'en and let me go home straightaway.

On my third season I was hired out to Phil Rodgers – Phil Beag. I had a bit of bad luck that year – I got a whitlow in my finger and it had to be lanced by the doctor. Dr Smyth was on duty at that time; he held his surgery in Arranmore once a week. I wasn't fit to do a tap of work; there was nothing I could do about it – I had to spend a fortnight at home until my finger healed. As soon as it was better, back I went to Phil's house to finish the term I was contracted for.

And what were my duties? Well, just like anywhere else there was housework to be done, and twenty other kinds of work besides. At that time of the year the men of the island went out fishing day after day, and the women of the house were busy washing for them. As well as that, the women would often spend the whole day working on the shore and I had to go along with them; when I didn't, I'd have to stay behind and do the housework, keep the children away from the tide or make sure they didn't go too near the fire. The women and the youngsters were gathering winkles, cutting dulse and corladdie (carrageen), working at the kelp or doing other kinds of work. The men were fishing lobsters up by Róninis or here and there in Boylagh Bay. There weren't all fishing, however, for early in the summer turf had to be cut out in Termon or Arranmore and brought back by boat to Iniskerragh.

Kelp-making was in full swing in my seasons on the island, and I was expected to help at that too. I've no need to tell you kelp-making was exhausting, tedious work from start to finish. A ton of kelp made between three and four pounds

Phil Óg Rodgers backing his boat ashore after a summer day's fishing off Iniskerragh; the boat will be pulled up and secured for the night on the strand. In the background: the Clocha Beannachta, Béal an Éilín and Cloughcor – the south-east corner of Arranmore.

then, and they reckoned it took about five tons of seaweed to make one ton of kelp. Seaweed was washed ashore at times, especially while the sea was still rough after a gale, but most of the time it had to be cut with hooks.

It was cut with the big hook, or kelp hook as they call it in places. It was specially made for the job. It had a long shaft so that the man using it could dip it down in the water and cut the seaweed growing down on the seabed. They usually did this at low tide, for it was then easy to cut; the best time of all was low water in the spring tides. Seaweed floats to the surface as soon as it's cut and then it has to be loaded aboard the boat. After it was brought ashore, it was spread out on the stone fences nearby; it was turned a few times to make sure it was thoroughly dry. It was then heaped in cocks and left like that for three weeks before it was burned in the kiln.

Cutting seaweed was man's work, but the women played their part in all the other stages – the spreading, the turning, the drying out, the burning, and so on.

It was a rare day you wouldn't see smoke rising from the kelp kilns throughout the Rosses at that time – the kilns in Inishfree, Iniskerragh, Arranmore, Róninis, on the shore at Traighenagh and so on. When the kelp was made, it had to be taken by boat as far as Burtonport or Rutland Harbour, and sold there. Later on, a ship would arrive to take a cargo of kelp to Scotland. Kelp-making was always done during the summer; you couldn't do that sort of work any other time of the year.

People were so poverty-stricken in those days that some of them hadn't the faintest idea of ease or pleasure. On Christmas Day itself you'd see them out gathering whatever seaweed had been washed ashore overnight. They'd maybe use it to manure the soil round about St Brigid's Day or later on. Because they were harvesting the seaweed, Charley Stoupe, the landlord decreed that his tenants weren't to cut any seaweed except where the water was at least nine feet deep. A man was fined for cutting black seaweed on the western end of Arranmore; seven shillings he was fined. It was out near Bearney he was cutting it – Bearney's a wild and dangerous place.

During my time in Iniskerragh the tenants had to pay a

rent of fifty pounds: twenty-six for the use of the land and twenty-four for the use of the seashore – making kelp, picking winkles or shellfish, dulse and the like. That decree of Stoupe's was horrible, was evil. Remember, there was no quay, no slipway, nothing as convenient as that on the island; bringing turf, kelp or anything else into or out of the island was pure hardship, it was nothing but sheer slavery from one end of the year to the other.

Cutting seaweed was always dangerous; cutting tangled wrack was dangerous too. Sometime before the Famine two boats left Arranmore for a load of seaweed up at Illancrone. I'm not sure just what time of the year it was, but it might have been the tail end of winter or some time early in spring. It's likely the weather wasn't very promising the morning they set out; nevertheless, by sail or by oar, they kept on course for the island. The skies were threatening; in spite of that they did not intend to turn back. When they were rowing past Iniskerragh, the old men on the island came out on the shore, shouting warnings at them, bidding them go no further. But there was no stopping them – on they went. One of the boats did the wise thing: they cut their load of seaweed as fast as any load of seaweed was ever cut in Ireland, and then hurried home before the day turned bad. It was a different story with the other boat. They went on loading more and more seaweed until it was too late to think of returning. The sea got up, and then the snow came on them – it was so heavy they couldn't find their way back. The boat and the fishermen were lost. I'd say their boat was a small one, there was probably just the two men in it. According to the story handed down to us, one of them was Seán Ward from the Illion; the widow's name was Máire. Their bodies were never recovered, but were reports that

Working on the shore on the mainland.

one of the corpses was washed ashore on the west coast of Scotland.

I'll let the poet finish the story:

Scairteach mhór mhór á déanamh in Árainn
ag iarraidh orainne na cladaí a fhágáil.
Ach imigí sibhse, nó is sibh atá sásta!
Ní chorróimidinne go raibh lasta den leathach linn.

Great and loud were the cries from Arran,
appealing to us as we pulled away from the shore.
Well, be off with you then, if that's what'll please you
We'll never turn back until our boat's is kelp filled.

A Mháire bhán bhocht, is tú béal na céille,
mo chailín stuama dá bhfuil de mhná in Éirinn.
Tá tú sa bhaile anocht agus nach dubh clár d'éadain,
is go bhfuil a fhios ag an tsaol mhór gur do chlann a thréig
      thú.

Poor white-haired Máire, you're on everyone's tongue now,
no sounder a woman can be found throughout Erin.
At home night by night, your brow dark with worry
sure the whole world knows how your family has deserted
      you.

Chuir bean chupaí in iúl do Mháire
go mbeadh siad chuici ar thús na mbádaí.
Ach chrom sí a ceann agus rinne sí foighid Dé
agus ar dheireadh gach scéala bhí an báthadh déanta.

By reading tea leaves the woman told Máire
they'd be back to her soon on the first boats.
She bowed her head low, with the patience of God,
for every report confirmed the drowning at sea.

Crews from Arranmore and the mainland often went out to cut kelp in Roninis, the tiny island out off Gweebarra Bay. They'd build huts for themselves and spend the summer there fishing and working at the kelp. Others came from Arranmore to Iniskerragh to do the same there too. Among those who went across one year were two Arranmore girls from Ploghogue – Caitlín Bhán and Bidí Róisín. They worked at the kelp at Rinnanean in Iniskerragh. They gathered a fair amount of it and put a lot of hard work into it – bringing it ashore, spreading it on walls to dry it out, building it in cocks and so on. They were well pleased with the great effort they had made, and there'd be no need now to burn the kelp for another week or two. Every day they were delighted to look across at the fruit of their labour. But a westerly gale blew up one night and not so much as a single cock of their kelp was left on the shore; it was all swept out to sea, and was gone with the tide forever; there wasn't a trace of Biddy and Caitlín's hard work. When Caitlín arose in the morning, she looked across at Iniskerragh; not a cock of their kelp could she see. And here's the lament she made on her loss:

> A leacacha Rinn na nÉan, sibh a bhuairigh mo cheann,
> tá mo sholáthar beag bliana ar shiúl leis an toinn,
> is níl dada le déanamh anois agam ach éaló liom.

> Oh rocks of Rinnanean, it's you that madden my mind.
> All my short season's labour swept away on the wind,
> and not a thing here for me now I will leave Rinnanean behind.

Of course the incident wasn't a total disaster for a few years later she married a man by the name of Dominick Molloy. Her friend that worked at the kelp with her, Bidí Róisín, married Taig Ward and they had a son called Seán Taig. Caitlín herself had two daughters, Biddy and Máire. And here's a remarkable thing: myself and Caitlín's Biddy were married on the very same day.

Five years ago everybody left Iniskerragh. Even though a living could still be made there, the young folk were determined to stay there no longer. They hadn't a priest, they had neither doctor nor nurse, and there were times they hadn't a schoolteacher; in their opinion they'd be far better off leaving Iniskerragh for good, and settling down somewhere else. They were unhappy about travelling to Arranmore for mass every Sunday, and that too wasn't possible if the sea was up. There wasn't even the electric light or a telephone on the island, and every summer there was the dreadful hardship of cutting the turf and ferrying it back to the island. Faced with all that, the young ones felt it was time to call it a day, time to quit the island, and that's what they did in 1955.

WORKING IN THE LAGAN

Apart from my time at Illion and across in Iniskerragh, I had hardly hired anywhere else until I travelled to the Lagan at the age of thirteen. After my three seasons on Iniskerragh I decided to go down to Tyrone. In the meantime I had to think about getting a few bits of clothes for when I was going away, so you can be sure I was delighted to earn a few more shillings the winter before I'd leave.

Sergeant Connolly and his wife needed a servant girl and my mother asked me to work there for a month or six weeks. The sergeant came from the Aran Islands in Galway, and I got to know him in the RIC barracks in Pollawaddy. There was a total of eight policemen in the barracks at that time. The sergeant married Nora O'Donnell, daughter of Johnny Hughdáin – the big shot who owned 'the wee house by the side of the road' at Leabgarrow – the house that's mentioned in Peadar Breathnach's song. Again and again people remarked on the dowry Johnny Hughdáin – gave with each of his daughters – one hundred pounds! That was a huge sum of money in those days.

During this winter I'm talking about the sergeant's wife wasn't at all well, and since they happened to have a sickly child, Mrs Connolly asked my mother if I'd do the housework for a while and look after the children too. I was more than

Two views of Burtonport Station. The train is ready to depart for Letterkenny and Derry. This line was closed down in 1940.

happy to do that, and I still remember the lovely shawl I bought for myself with the money. I had a shawl at the time of course, but it was long past time for a new one, for the shawl I had on me was one that had seen plenty wear: it was Kitty's, and she had passed it on to me after spending two seasons down in Strabane. This new shawl of mine meant a great deal to me, for unlike any article of clothing I had worn so far it was something I had bought myself. It goes without saying I remember every detail as if it was yesterday I bought it. A Shepherd's Plaid it was, and my mother was with me that day in Keon's Shop in Burtonport. It was only eight shillings, and I wore it the day I set out for the Lagan all those years ago.

The hiring fairs in Strabane were held on Old Hallowe'en (12 November) and Old May Day (12 May). Those were two big days in the life of the young ones then; they were every bit as important as Christmas Day and Easter Sunday are for children these days. I went down to the May hiring, and a neighbour of ours – Róise McGinley from Leabgarrow – was my companion on the journey.

On the morning I left home I was up and about from early on. We had to go out on the post boat to Burtonport, and after that we'd have to walk as far as Dungloe. Néill Neansaí's people had the contract for ferrying the post to and from the island, and they didn't charge me a penny for the journey. On the boat there was this old woman, and when she learned I was going to the Lagan, she took great pity on me and began advising me about this and that. I listened attentively, even though I'd heard the selfsame advice a hundred times the week before. As for blessed objects, you can be sure my mother didn't send me away without seeing to that: rosary beads, a little prayer book she had bought for me at the mission, two little bottles – one with holy water, the other with water from Doon Well – I had the lot; she didn't forget a thing.

It was never in God's plan that I should have children of my own, and from time to time, I'd worry about that and I'd be

Burtonport Harbour 1905.

on the verge of grumbling and griping and complaining to God. I'd say every woman in the world the same as me would feel like complaining too – it's only natural. But then I'd start remembering my poor mother the night before I left home, bound for Tyrone far away. There she was, sitting by the fire busily stitching a blessed medal and an *Agnus Dei* onto the clothes I'd be wearing in the land of the strangers; different ideas would come into my head then, and soon I'd find peace of mind. God's will be done. He alone knows what is best for all of us. We've no right to be complaining.

In Dungloe I met a girl my own age; she too was going down to the Lagan, and travelling with her cheered me up. She came from the mainland, from Clogherdillure in the Rosses; her name was Anne Boyle, Anna Jimmy Bhoy – she was the best of company. I hadn't the slightest idea who she was before that day, but after we were in each other's company

Above and opposite: Burtonport Harbour today. Between 1975 and 1980 the harbour was extended.

an hour or two, you'd imagine we were lifelong neighbours. Her people were blacksmiths, and the people of Arranmore often went out to them to get them to make anchors, rudders, horseshoes and the like in their forge. I had planned to walk the whole way to Ballybofey, but Anna wouldn't hear of it. She was a lot cuter, more worldly-wise than me, and told me we would get there on the mail car. At that time Johndy Bán Sweeney's people had the mail contract to Ballybofey, and that's how we left Dungloe. The Sweeneys of Dungloe owned the sidecar, Patrick Sweeney, Páidí Shéamais Óig, was the driver; he came from Acres, and was Anna's next-door neighbour; she knew him well.

Anna and I sat up on the car and handed the driver our small bundles; he stored them in the 'well' – the baggage compart-

ment. There was just the four of us: Anna and myself on one side and two boys from Annagary on the other. That sidecar is what's known as a jaunting car and the driver sat up on the 'dicky', the seat in the middle at the front. Paddy stopped a couple of minutes at Doochary to give us a chance to buy a poke of lozenges. We bought a pennyworth each, and we felt the woman of the shop had given us good value. I didn't know her name that day, but I got to know her well later on – Gráinne Mhór of Doochary.

The driver charged us two shillings apiece for the journey down to Ballybofey. The roads were awful and it was difficult to travel on them in any sort of carriage. They were topped with big stones, and there were potholes from one end of the road to the other. When we were on our way the driver told us the road wasn't bad that day – you should see what it's like in winter, he said. All the same, it would be hard to find a major county road anywhere in Ireland as bad as that one. The driver didn't stop anywhere apart from exchanging a word or two with carters from Burtonport; they were on their way back from Ballybofey with groceries for shopkeepers in the Rosses. There was no rail track to Fintown or Burtonport – indeed it would be a long time before the line ran as far as those places, and these men, Jimmy Condy Ruaidh, Niall Eoghanín O'Donnell and Paddy Charlie Boyle, were doing that journey twice a week and returning with a full load to the Rosses.

I was delighted to travel on the sidecar, for my boots were hurting me and I hadn't worn them to the shape of my foot yet. They were a new pair; Charlie Hunter, the shoemaker in Cruickamore, Dungloe, had made them for me a short while before this. In my small bundle of clothes I had a skirt of green wool my mother had made the week before I left. She made the whole skirt on her own from first to last. She began by carding the wool into rolls, and then spun it into thread; Charlie Gallagher, in Ploghogue, wove it on his loom and made her a web of cloth; she cut out the different parts, and finally sewed all the pieces together.

I don't know how long it took us to get to Ballybofey; we seemed to be on the road a very long time that day, but then the like of that didn't annoy people a lot in those days – there were no motor cars or buses. But I do know we were famished by the time we reached the town; speaking for myself, I was like somebody who had crossed 'hungry grass' or 'fear gorta' after a long summer's day work at the turf above on the hill in Arranmore.

Anyone who ever travelled that road will know the steep slopes we had to climb. The driver said the poor horse mightn't be fit for it with the four of us on the sidecar, so he asked us to get off at the worst slopes and walk to the top of the brae.

That was sound advice; on the road out from Doochary we could see that the horse was starting to get tired, so we took to our feet at The Sceardán and The Carbad and the climb at Glenfinn; that gave the poor beast a bit of ease.

We spent the night in Ballybofey, and in the morning we'd be travelling on the train to Strabane. When we were saying goodbye to Paddy, the driver, he told us where to go for our lodgings – Mrs McLaughlin's; and that's where we stayed the night; she only charged us a shilling apiece. There were sixteen of us all looking for somewhere to stay, but Mrs McLaughlin had only room for four; the others had to find somewhere else in the town. Anna Jimmy Bhoy and myself were now as thick as thieves and we took two others with us into our lodgings – my neighbour from the island, Róise McGinley, and a boy from the mainland – Anna's brother – Donncha Jimmy Bhoy. You couldn't find fault with that house of Mrs McLaughlin's; our beds were very good and she gave us our fill to eat, and in the morning we got a full bowl of milk and plenty of oaten bread as well.

So we were well pleased as we left for Strabane. There was a big crowd of us and, believe me, we were full of fun and high-spirits. We were young and on top of the world, yelling and jumping about as we set off on the road. You'd have said we were schoolchildren heading home on our holidays after a long term's work. You can never snuff out the liveliness of youth.

The train ran from Stranorlar to Strabane, and to make sure we'd be in time for the fair we took the first one in the morning. Mrs McLaughlin made sure to get us up early; even so, by the time we reached the station there were crowds waiting for the train to leave. Those of us from Arranmore weren't the only ones there – there were boys and girls the same age as ourselves from all parts of the West Donegal, from Glenties, Ardara, Glenfinn, the Rosses and places with names I'd never heard tell of till that day. Never had I seen so many young ones together. The ticket cost one shilling and six pence, and the train was so full there weren't seats for half of us. The journey took three-quarters of an hour, so we were in Strabane an hour before the fair started – people were only beginning to arrive for it. It wasn't long before we were hired for the season. We were cocky and happy in ourselves; we much more at our ease now with every one of us getting a place.

After we had something in an eating-house, we walked around the town looking in shop windows and marvelling at all the things to be seen. There were lots of horses and carts; the farmers had arrived in the town that morning to hire boys or girls for the half year. The horses weren't harnessed to the carts or traps but were tethered in the square; a bundle of hay was thrown to them while their masters went about their business in the town. As is always the custom at fairs, there were people there providing entertainment and diversion – singers, fiddlers, hawkers of every kind, trick-o'-the-loop men, and so on – never in my life had I seen such a huge crowd, and we were free to drink all the fun and the joy of the day now that we'd been hired.

Around five in the afternoon we all went to the market house and we stayed there for an hour or so until our new masters came to take us home with them. I still remember what we were talking about and us standing there. There wasn't any homesickness or anxiety at that stage – it was too early to be affected by the like of that, but it would come later on in the day. Everyone was telling everybody else where they were going, and also asking others what places they had got: 'Where are you for, yourself?' Donemana, or Omagh, Murlog, Gortin, Glenmornan, or some other strange place with names I'd never heard of before. They called us the 'ignoramuses' – the greenhorns! – we were new to the Lagan, and we had to depend on the older ones to tell us this and that. And as for ourselves, where were we going? Róise McGinley was going to a farmer near Donemana, Anna Jimmy Bhoy somewhere near Sion Mills, and I was hired to a farm in Glenmornan.

I was quite pleased with the place I got – Mrs McGee's of Glenmornan. They were Catholics; that was a help, for they knew all about my religion, something, perhaps, you mightn't find with people of a different creed. Having said that, I have come across people of my own age who said they always preferred to be hired out to Protestants. Protestants and Presbyterians, they said, don't do as much work on Sundays as the Catholics and on account of that there was always a rest for them on the Lord's Day. There was a certain amount of truth in that. Anyway, the McGees were Catholics and they were very well off. The man of the house was about sixty; his wife, I'd say, wasn't much more than a third his age.

I wasn't the first Arranmore girl to work on their farm. Hannah Rua McAuley, Hannah Charlie Sheáin from Aphort, was there before me, and further back still Hannah's aunt – Nancy Sheáin – had worked for the McGees. She was working there a long time before she married a man from that district, Michael Herron. Here's an interesting fact about Seán McAuley – Hannah's grandfather: he had seven daughters in his family but only one son – Charlie. It was widely believed that the youngest of those daughters had a cure for scrofula or the Evil, as the Rosses people called it.

Hannah Rua went to Scotland and later to America. There she married one of the Boyles of Screig an tSeabhaic. Many years later they returned to Ireland and bought The Glen House, 'The Big House' that once belonged to John Stoupe Charley, the landlord. It's now called the Glen Hotel; Hannah and Jack have been running it these past thirty years.

I was promised only three pounds fifteen shillings by the McGees for the half year. What sort of work did they expect of me for that money? Well, I had to do every kind of housework; helping out in the fields wasn't part of my duties; even so, I was seldom idle. I wore a sack apron all day long and had all sorts of hard work to do – scouring tubs, scrubbing the pantry, dashing milk, and so on. They had a 'horse churn'. The churn was placed in the middle of a house and the horse plodded round in a circle; and as he walked, the churn revolved for there was a shaft on the churn and it was chained to the horse's harness; that's the way they turned the churn, the horse doing the walking round and round. I had never seen anything like it; that churn was amazing. The only churn my mother ever had at home was a small one with a staff for dashing the milk; it wasn't very big and we only used it in summer when we had plenty of milk. Mrs McGee's churn held a huge amount of milk and it was my job to help her churn it, but as soon as I got the hang of it, she left me to do the whole job. As I said, harnessing the horse and so on wasn't part of my duties – they had a servant boy to lead the horse into the churning-house and he'd walk round and round with the horse on the reins. The same horse was easy handled, a wise old animal kept for that job, and he walked the circuit quietly and peaceably – it's what he'd been doing year in, year out. When the churning was finished, I had to scoop the butter together and lift it out of the churn; the vessels and the churn had then to be scalded and washed, the butter had to be made up and left in the pantry, the pantry had to be tidied after all that work, and on it went, on and on ...

Mrs McGee herself treated me fairly well; she brought me a nice ribbon from Strabane one day and on a Sunday she'd help me dress up for mass. When I finished my half-year, they gave me five pounds and ten shillings, even though they could have sent me off with the three pounds fifteen shillings we had agreed on.

I hadn't far to go to mass on Sundays, for there were two chapels near McGee's – Glenmornan and Cloghcor. I was only half a mile from the chapel in Glenmornan, so I usually went there. At that time we were only allowed to mass every other Sunday. Fr Connolly was the Glenmornan priest at that time, and he was known far and wide for his saintliness. I went to him for confession many a time; my English wasn't good, but I'd say he knew that from the way he talked to me. At all times he'd do his utmost for every poor creature.

Now and again I'd go to Cloghcor even though it meant a longer walk – an extra two miles. There was a lovely priest there too – Fr Scanlon. To this day I can recall the nice way he spoke to me and the other hired children. There was a mission in Cloghcor during my time in McGee's, and I did my best to attend the ceremonies. I've always been very fond of music, so I tried my best to join in when ever the choir was singing the hymns; that's something I always did wherever I happened to be. And I remember Fr Scanlon started talking to me one day outside the chapel. He wanted to find out as much as he could about me, my name, where I was hired, my people at home, where it was they lived in the 'back country', and lots of other things as well. I was surprised how well he knew the 'back country' – the name the Tyrone people used when talking about West Donegal.

My sister Kitty was hired not too far from me, and on Sundays we'd meet at Glenmornan chapel. It goes without saying we were delighted to get a chance to talk to each other and chew over any news we might have heard from home. Kitty was older than me and, as you'd expect, she'd have the most of whatever was going. There was just one other girl I knew to see there – Bríd Rodgers from Leabrannagh; I always met her too at the gate after mass.

Time passed and the November Fair was now upon us. I had to make up my mind about what was best for me: should I stay on in Tyrone for the winter, or go home for the next six months and remain there till the next hiring-fair, 12 May. I ended up staying on in Tyrone, didn't go home at all. Kitty had landed a good place for me at Milltown in Artigarvan, a couple of miles outside Strabane; as it wasn't often a girl of my age could get as good a station as that, I decided not to move away from the area. I wrote to my mother and sent her what I had earned in my six months at McGee's. Postage stamps were only a penny then; I kept a shilling for stamps for the letters I'd send home; I didn't put any money by for myself until I was eighteen years of age.

I then went to work for Dr Boyd from Lifford who owned this farm at Milltown; he had a manager and some others to look after it. Dan Ferry was the manager; his wife, Kitty, wasn't in good health however; she never went out much – in fact, she kept to her bed most of the time. There were forty head of cattle on the farm, sturdy stock, bullocks, heifers and so on; in winter the cattle had to be kept and foddered indoors and the stockman, John Smyth, saw to that. They were never short of anything in that farmhouse; Dr Boyd made sure they had plenty of potatoes, vegetables, everything like that. Dan Ferry – the man of the house – liked to look well, and that meant still more work for me. He had up to half a dozen pairs of boots, and every week without fail it was my job to clean and polish them. And that wasn't all: I had to have half a dozen shirts ready for him every week too. On top of this I had the housework to do, and a cow to look after as well, the cow that kept the house in milk.

I'll never forget that cow. She was a big and brindled, and gave four times as much milk as any cow I had seen so far. The first time I'd go to the byre I'd bring two large pails with me – those pails with the circular rims. I'd milk the full of the two pails, and carry them into the pantry; I'd strain the milk and pour it into the large crockery jars we stored the milk in. I'd go out with the third pail and she'd fill that too. In summer I had to churn the milk twice a week – Saturdays and Mondays. If I tried to limit it to the one churning, the jars and basins couldn't hold all the milk she yielded. The churn they had was a large, high one and I'd move it to the middle of the floor. I had to stand on a chair in order to dash the milk; that chair had to be a stout one – the seat was made from thick wooden boards. I'd stand up there, grip the plunger, and dash and dash until the fat broke out in the milk. It was brutally hard work, and I couldn't get anybody else to help me. Summer was the worst time; there was just the one churning a week in the other seasons. I quit this house after putting in the six months – another farm offered me one pound and five shillings more than I was getting there.

The new farmhouse was only half a mile away. My employer was Robert McCombe – a very wealthy farmer of the district.

The McCombes were Presbyterians, and they had two farms, one in Milltown, the other in Grianlach; the farms were no distance from each other. Mr McCombe had heard about me for I'd been working in the neighbourhood for the past half year. He approached me at the hiring fair in Strabane and offered me seven pounds and five shillings for the half year. There was no haggling – I said I'd go and welcome. My sisters, Máire and Kitty, had worked for him before this, and it's there Kitty kept on working till she married Patrick McNulty, a native of the district. They had thirteen of a family. Kitty's dead now a long time; she's buried down there in County Tyrone. As I've mentioned already, Máire had worked for Mr McCombe, she had spent three seasons there.

You can be sure I was given tons of work in my time at Robert McCombe's. His wife was one of the Knoxs of Derry of Colmcille; she was an extremely beautiful woman. They had six children – John, Willy, Margaret, Julia, Anna and Evelyn. They were still very young, but they were well brought up, and they'd never turn the word in your mouth. In addition to all our inside and outside jobs there were two big tubs of washing to be done every week. Mrs McCombe was pleasant and friendly, and a first class worker. I spent two half-years with the McCombes; if she hadn't been so nice to me, I'd only have stayed a single season there.

During my time with the McCombes I attended mass in the same chapels, for I was still working in that neighbourhood, even though I changed house a couple of times; so it was either Glenmornan or Cloghcor I went to. Another lovely priest arrived whom I got to know, Fr Joseph Convery; I believe he said he was from County Derry. My employers, as I said, were Presbyterians and I could see they knew very little about

Sheskinarone in 1987.

my religion. And as I said earlier, we were allowed to go to mass every other Sunday. Since I was going to receive Holy Communion, I used to fast on the Sundays I'd go to mass. The mistress of the house must have noticed this, for – what do you think – she approached me one day on that very point and asked me why I hadn't eaten my breakfast. I had to tell her about the rule we had – the rule about 'fasting from midnight the night before'. She confessed this was all new to her, she hadn't the least notion of it up to then.

They had fourteen milking cows, and it was our job – myself and the mistress of the house – to milk them, carry the milk into the pantry, strain it, and later pour it into the churn. Theirs was a horse churn too; our duties were the same as those I talked about earlier in McGee's.

Having spent two seasons in McCombe's in Grianlach, I left County Tyrone and came to Donegal, my own county. I went to Robertson's on the banks of Lough Swilly. His farm was in the Manorcunningham district facing Lough Swilly and the hills of Inishowen. Andrew Robertson had only recently arrived there – he had bought the farm from Glendennon. He paid me seven pounds for the first six months, but seven pounds and ten shillings for the next two seasons. There's no question about it – I had a huge amount of work to get through on that farm, outdoors as well as indoors. Those Lagan farmers wrung the last drop of energy out of us and, God knows, it was little enough they paid us. As I said already, we had a fierce amount to do, and we were still only youngsters.

There was a great acreage of flax around Manor, and Robertson had a mill to meet the needs of the farmers; every year they'd send him their flax for threshing. Like the McCombes of Grianlach, he had fourteen milking cows, and the cream was sold to the Sallybrook Creamery. Every day the creamery cans came back filled to the brim with skimmed milk; those cans had to be emptied into tubs; six bucketfuls of that milk, with a bowl of linseed meal mixed into it, were fed to the calves twice a day – after breakfast and again in the evening.

Mrs Robertson's maiden name was Thompson, and a brother of hers – John Thompson – was the lord mayor of Derry of Colmcille at that time; their mother was one of the Keons of Bunbeg.

When I was there I always went to mass in Newtowncunningham. There was only one other person from the Rosses working in that area – Kitty O'Donnell from Brockagh near Dungloe. We'd meet after mass. Her father was Laoise O'Donnell, and her mother, Fanny Frank Owen Bhig, came from Purt Inish Mil, Burtonport. An aunt of hers lived in Arranmore, and we had first come across each other when we were children, for Kitty used to come in and visit her aunt's family on the island.

Having spent three half-years working for Andrew Robertson on the banks of Lough Swilly I came up to Arranmore in November, and stayed home that winter. I'd been a long time in the Lagan and my mother felt it was time I had a rest. From the very first day we went to the Lagan we worked very hard, and I was now getting tired of it. My stepsister, Nancy, wrote to me, urging me to come up home. There was nothing in the Lagan but heavy, slavish work for a meagre amount of money. They made us get up at six in the morning, and we were still on our feet late at night. Not only that, the food was seldom up to the mark. In her letter – it arrived just as I was about to leave Robertson's – Nancy said I'd be much better off if I went to Scotland, and she told me not to go back to the Lagan again. I took her advice and came up to Arranmore. I was glad to be home again.

Glad as I was, my mother was crazy with delight. She hugged me and kissed me and cried out: 'My heart's treasure! At last you're back here with me!' And then she burst into a flood of tears from the sheer joy of having me home.

THE KNITTING

Now that I was home for the winter I had to find something to do over the next six months, something that would pass the time and help me earn some money for myself and for the others in the family. What I earned during my time in the Lagan was a help for it gave me a chance to put aside a couple of pounds I wouldn't have been able to have it if I'd stayed at home, and with that I bought boots and clothes for myself. People often criticised seasonal migration and sneered at it, but think how badly off we'd be without it – we would have had absolutely nothing to keep us alive. And so, in spite of the joy we felt when we came home now and again for the winter, we well knew what lay ahead of us. Even on the best of days it was obvious there was nothing but hunger and poverty there. We would have had nothing but the few pennies that were dear bought. Now and again during the winter the men and the young lads had the fishing, but what was there for the women and the girls? There was little for them apart from the odd shilling they'd earn from knitting. And, believe me, earning that money was real hardship. As the women said, it was won through their very bones. No wonder the old women in the Rosses long ago had a name for the needles between their fingers – 'the four crowbars of poverty' – as they toiled and toiled at the knitting!

Of course it wasn't today or yesterday the knitting started in this part of the country. The Búistéir – God rest him – was a knowledgeable man; he was of the opinion there had always been knitting here. That's certainly true, but when was it women first started knitting for money? He couldn't answer that, and for her part my mother remembered they had been knitting for money all the years she was growing up. From what the Búistéir said, he could never remember a time when they weren't knitting stockings for the British soldiers, and I think he was correct in that. It was for Queen Victoria's soldiers they were knitting those stockings, and the only name the women ever gave the yarn was 'the queen's wool'. The very old queen was still alive while I was growing up, and I was just a year or two over twenty when we heard word of her death.

Long ago those were the stockings the women of the Rosses made for McDevitts in Glenties. The McDevitts were as prosperous a clan as you'd find in Ireland. There was nothing in the world they didn't own – they had great big mansions, shops, lots of land, horses and coaches, and so on. They were noted for their wealth throughout the country.

Anyone who wanted knitting wool had to get it in Glenties. It is every inch of twenty-one miles from Burtonport to Glenties, and the Arranmore women and the women of the mainland with their little bundles of socks had that distance to walk every fortnight; whatever they had knit would be sold there, and if their work was satisfactory, they'd be given more wool for the next fortnight. Walking as far as Glenties wasn't too strenuous if the weather was fine, but think of the hardship those women endured with six inches of snow on the road ahead of them; think of it raining cats and dogs, or think of a day with a fierce gale blowing in your face! The journey

Embroidery classes for young girls. Certain landlords and business people established classes like these for the good of the public and, no doubt, for their own profit too.

up and the journey back down again in conditions like that caused them shocking pain and misery.

At the start, they could only get the wool in McDevitts itself. Years later, however, when they began to realise the rigour the women suffered on the long walk, they gave out the wool closer to home – in Lettermacaward. Even so, Lettermacaward was a long hard walk for them. It's likely McDevitts never thought of sending the wool as far as the Rosses on a sidecar and bringing the finished work back to Glenties later in the day. I'd go so far as to say they did perhaps think of doing that, but those people lost no sleep over the hardship they inflicted on the women. As the saying has it – Mr Comfort doesn't recognise Mr Lean.

Bad as the long walk was for the women of the mainland, it was far, far worse for the women from Arranmore. They had to leave by boat in the morning so they were late starting out on the walk. And if they returned late from Glenties they had to find lodgings in Burtonport: no boat would take them back at night.

My sister Máire usually walked to Lettermacaward with her neighbour Róise McGinley. They made sure to have everything ready for their tea on the way up and on their way down again. They'd buy a half-ounce of tea, four ounces of sugar and two small scones, a penny apiece, so that they'd have two meals in the course of the day. They'd have their meal in a house on the way. They were very late getting back to Burtonport one night – it was between ten and twelve o'clock, and they didn't know where they might find lodgings. At that time the biggest houses in Burtonport were Sweeney's (Jim Johndy's house) and Keon's – both places were shops as well as dwelling houses. Peggy Micheál Caitlín from Iniskerragh was a servant girl in Sweeney's; she knew the two girls, so they told her their problem and urged her to ask the owners of the house if they'd allow them sleep by the fire overnight. The Sweeneys said they were very welcome to, so they made pillows of their bundle of wool and slept on the floor right through to the morning; they had no trouble sleeping that night after their long walk that day. There were other Arranmore women as well on the road that day; they spent the night in Denis Boner's house in Acres nearby.

There were two types of yarn for the knitters then – the rough and the fine. McDevitt used to pay three shillings and six pence for a dozen socks of the rough yarn and five shillings and six pence for a dozen of the fine. Knitting them was fairly hard work – remember, there were only small lamps in the houses; knitting after nightfall was difficult.

The most prosperous of the McDevitt clan – the man called Hugh – left thousands of pounds behind him when he died. In his will he set aside a huge sum for a college to be established in Glenties, where the young people in West Donegal could be educated. I believe at the end of his day his conscience got the better of him – he felt obliged to educate those people that had helped him make so much money through their knitting. The school he founded – *The McDevitt Institute* – is still there today.

I've mentioned the woman from Ploghogue, Caitlín Ban already; she's the woman who composed the verses after she lost the kelp in Iniskerragh long ago. Like everyone one else Caitlín went to Glenties with her little bundle of stockings. One of those days when she was up there, it seems as if she wasn't going to get away soon enough. In charge of the shop was Mickey the Yarn-man, and it wasn't likely he'd do them any favours and let them away early. Thinks Caitlín Ban to herself: 'I'll have a go at a verse or two that might make him aware of the people from the island.' She began praising the people in the shop, those who supplied the yarn, hinting that she and the others might be back in Burtonport before nightfall and, hopefully, arrive home before dark:

A Dhálaigh, a dhuine uasail, a bhfuil do chine i ngach uile áit,
is de do chine mise, is ní shéanfaidh mé é go brách.
Má fheiceann tú muintir Árann, tabhair daofa uilig snáth.
Má choinníonn tú go mall iad, imeochaidh orthu an bád.
Is dá dtriomaíodh Béal Árann, bheadh sin acu bealach réidh.

O'Donnell, noble sir, 'tis everywhere your clan's to be found.
I come from your clan too – a truth I will never deny.

See those women from Arran – hand out your thread to
them one and all.
Should you hold them back too long, the boat'll take off
without them.
Of course if Arran Roads dried up, they would have a handy
way home!

Agus tusa, a Charlie Kennedy, níor mhol mé thú ar dóigh.
Bheirim seoid an chruinnithe duit, is tú féin an buachaill
cóir.
Go bhfaighe tú bean mhaith dhathúil, a mbeidh aici mámaí
óir,
Is má thabhrann do mhuintir tuilleadh duit, nach ort a bheas
an dóigh!

And you, Charlie Kennedy, sure I didn't do you justice at all.
You're the jewel of the crowd, a prime and a decent young
man!
May you win a fine, comely woman, one who's got heaps of
gold,
Your own will add more to it – yes, you'll be on the pig's back!

Biddy Caitlín, Caitlín Ban's daughter, did the knitting for her
mother, and her just a wee girl at the time. Caitlín Ban, it must
be said, never missed a chance to praise her daughter:

Dá bhfeicfeá an tseoid a rínne iad,
chuirfeadh sí sin ort bród,
agus an áit ar dhearc tú uilig orthu,
amuigh i mbarr na mbróg.

If you saw the fine needlework she did,
your heart it would burst with pride.
And where was it seen at its best?
In the overlap at the top of the boot.

We don't know if Caitlín's sweet-talk worked in McDevitts

that day, but I'd say it didn't do her any harm either. Those verses of hers have been recited again and again ever since then.

As well as knitting stockings for McDevitts, the women had to knit hats, jerseys, under-clothes and the like for their own families; they dyed them with bluestone; sometimes they bought the dye at home, sometimes in Scotland or down in the Lagan.

Too much knitting in poor light often damaged their eyes; they'd try to finish the piece they were working at after darkness had fallen and that was sore on them. I can manage bright or green wool nowadays, but don't ask me to knit dark yarn – least of all the blue, the black or the brown.

In the past it was the custom for elderly people to wear glasses if they happened to be working by night or at times during the day. The women would wear spectacles when they were sewing or knitting, and the men would wear them when they were repairing nets or doing things like that. Glasses were cheap then, and they weren't hard to get either. Men would come round the houses with them in the summertime. I remember the time the man came into the Búistéir's house years and years ago; he had a large pack of spectacles for the old people in the area, and he opened out the pack in the middle of the floor. I couldn't tell you how many pairs of specs he had. My mother and the Búistéir both needed specs, and it was God surely directed that man to the house. He had a newspaper with a lot of pictures on it – that was his test card for anyone needing glasses. I know my mother and the Búistéir tried up to a dozen until they found a pair that suited them. And they weren't dear at all – two shillings or a half-crown each. This day I'm talking about there wasn't an old man or an old woman in the district that didn't buy a pair of spectacles.

Thank God, we now have the electric light on the island and it's a great benefit to everyone, young and old. The children have no bother doing their homework after nightfall, and the woman of the house can enjoy doing her housework. God rest the faithful departed, wouldn't they be amazed and delighted if they came back from the dead today! They'd be singing the praises of all the changes that have come about.

For my own part I must say my eyesight's been poor a long time back, and that's not surprising, for I did a lot of sewing and knitting in my time. Early in my life, just like everyone else I was knitting for 'the man in Glenties', and even in the years I was working at the potatoes I'd bring some yarn of my own, or I'd make a point of buying it across in Scotland; if a bad day kept us in off the fields, I'd have a chance to knit stockings for my mother and the Búistéir back home. All through our life we were seldom idle. That was the lesson we learned from our mother at the fireside long ago. And when I got married and had my own house to look after, there was lots of knitting to be done as well. Every summer, when my husband set off for Scotland, I'd have to make sure there were a dozen pairs of stockings ready for him. At other times I'd send him a couple of pairs with someone who'd be leaving later on in the season.

And again, when there wasn't much to be done in the house and I was on my own, I'd go off and knit for other people here and there on the island. Some women with large families, who hadn't a chance to do their own knitting, would come to me and ask me to knit a pair of socks or a jersey or a beret for their children at school. That's how I spent my life. Instead of sitting and gazing into the fire I kept on working. We always did our utmost – God won't be too sore on us.

THE LIFE WE HAD

In the years before the Famine it was only now and again the priest stayed on the island. On Sundays he'd come in from the mainland, celebrate the mass and in the afternoon he'd be away back again. He'd also come in twice a year for the stations. There was one time the priest was to say the stations in the middle of the island, at Ballard in Ballintra. Since there wasn't a parochial house on the island nor a hotel, the house the stations was to be held had to put up the priest for the night. So, according to the custom of the time that's where the priest was given his night's lodgings. It seems this priest hadn't a clock or a timepiece of any kind, and of course the man of the house in Ballard didn't have one either. The priest was afraid he mightn't wake up in time for mass in the morning. He asked the housewife had she a rooster; no, she hadn't a rooster either.

But the priest wasn't beaten. After they had said the rosary everyone in the house went to bed; the priest, however, stayed up on his own. He went out to the nearest house in the neighbourhood and borrowed a cock to wake them up in the morning. He took the cock, put it under a large wicker creel outside the door and left a stone on the top of the creel to make sure the cock wouldn't budge until the morning. Well pleased with himself he slipped back into the house and went to bed. With the coming of daylight the rooster let forth so loud a screech it woke everyone out of their sleep. The woman of the house was amazed; she had no idea where the rooster had come from.

'Maybe there isn't a rooster outside there at all,' said she.

'Maybe it's a miracle the holy father himself's after performin' and him sleepin' the night under our own very roof.'

Priests in those days were terribly poor. There was no money coming to them apart from the little they'd get by way of the stipend; and it was little enough they got at funerals too. The Búistéir told me there was a funeral once where the whole offerings amounted to sixpence! Stipends were always collected at the autumn confessions; today's stipend is just four shillings and six pence per house. There was the odd house that never paid the stipend; they didn't pay offerings at the funerals either – in fact, they never paid anything at all.

There was this old woman in Arranmore a long time ago and one year she wasn't able to pay the stipend. She was living on her own; there was nobody to earn any money for her at all, she was as poor as a church mouse. The priest used to call for his stipend – but that's all he got for his trouble. One day he came to her house; it was the same old story as usual: there was no way could she pay even the tiniest portion of the stipend. He was about to leave the house, and maybe he was angry with her or maybe he wasn't, but anyway he pretended to be angry. On his way out an old clocking hen was pecking around the door, and he bent down as if he was about to snatch her up under his arm in place of the stipend.

'If you don't give me the stipend, I'll take her home with me,' he said. Standing at the half-door the old woman looked out at him – and she was the one that had the last word.

'Father,' said she, 'if you take that hen of mine away with you, you'll be worse than the devil himself. A hundred times a week that hen has been driving me mad – I can never keep her out of the house; again and again she's in here, poking and scraping all over the place. A hundred times I've begged the devil to take that hen away on me; it seems he didn't feel too happy to be doing the like of that. And now, just take a good look at yourself – taking my hen off with you in place of the stipend.'

The priest laughed and went off down the road. He never did get that stipend.

In the old days we just had plain, basic food. There was no butter apart from what we made ourselves. There was no creamery butter for sale in the shops, but people who had two milking cows would sell the butter they made through the shops, especially in summertime when there was plenty of milk. Every house had their own hens, and every week they sold the eggs. The egg money kept them in tea, sugar, pork, biscuits and other groceries. You could seldom buy bread in the shops. Some bread came on the Derry train long ago, but the extension to Burtonport didn't open until 1903. Indeed it was only recently in this century the grocery vans started making regular runs through the country, and that's when the shops began to sell 'white bread'.

It was some time in the first half of the last century that white flour first arrived in these parts. It was all oaten bread in my childhood. Again and again the old people used to say there was nothing better for quelling the hunger when you'd be out working at the turf in the summer than the oatmeal cake in your pocket.

Our way of life has improved greatly since I was a girl

– God be praised for all the changes that have come about – and it's not just in food only that things have taken a turn for the better. It must be emphasised that huge improvements have taken place in the houses the people live in. Any stranger or tourist will agree with me when I say that the houses in the Donegal Gaeltacht are as good as any you'll find throughout Ireland. They're a source of pride to us all. In my early years houses had no shape or style; most of them were just small thatched cabins with low roofs; there was only a kitchen and one other room.

Rome wasn't built in a day. There's truth in that proverb, it must be said, and it certainly applied to the houses long ago in the Rosses. When a man married and began to make his way in life, he'd build a house of some sort for himself and his wife. Usually he'd only build a thatched kitchen, and that provided them with a roof over their head for the time being. That kitchen was about twenty feet long and twelve feet broad, and there was just the single chimney. Inside the gable at the end opposite the two doors were the fireplace and the chimney. A tester or canopied bed was fitted into the outshot or recess close to the fire. There was just one window in the kitchen, a small one on the wall opposite the bed. Down at the other end of the kitchen were two doors, one in each side; one of them was left open if the wind was blowing against the other door; the door facing west wasn't often left open for that was the side that got the wind most.

Those houses weren't very high – the walls were just six feet or six and a half feet at the most. Building a house like that didn't take long – not much stone was needed. There was a further reason for the low walls: a house like that would catch a lot less wind. People liked to align their houses to the north or to the south-west: they reckoned a gale wouldn't do a lot of damage if the gable took the force of the wind. As well as that, if the house was thatched with straw or the bent grass that grows at the shore, it was felt the house ought to be angled in that direction: both sides of the roof would get the same amount of sunlight every day and the sun would dry the thatch evenly; that way the thatch would last a lot longer.

When I was young, the floor was covered with blue clay; cement floors or wooden floors came a lot later. There's no two ways about it – those blue clay floors were totally useless. It was hard keeping them clean, and it was hard as well to keep holes from being made in them by the legs of the iron pots. Brushes were made from heather in those days, and until fairly recently that was the usual sort of broom they brushed the floors with. The people who lived near the shore would carry up a bucket of clean sand and spread it on the floor; they did this on Saturdays so as to have a nice clean floor for Sunday.

The windows were small, with four very small panes in them. There was no sash, they couldn't be opened any day of the year, summer or winter. They didn't let in much sunlight either; to brighten the house the kitchen door was usually left open throughout the day, apart from days when the wind was strong or for some reason like that. Most houses had a full door and a half-door; the big door was left ajar, but the half-door was closed most of the time to let in the daylight and to keep out the hens! The walls were whitewashed and the inside was whitewashed too; as for paint, you'd see more paint in a single house today than would have been needed for the whole townland at that time; and, truth to tell, there wasn't enough furniture in those houses to warrant a lick of paint.

Thanks be to God, the electric light has come to the island. We never knew luxury until we got it. I still remember the misery we had to put up with for want of light at night. Most of the time all we had was a stump of bog-fir stuck in the fire. There was no shortage of that sort of light, for we lived on the edge of the bog and the Búistéir hadn't any trouble finding a root or a stump. We had a small oil lamp, but devil a bit use that was; its light was no stronger than the light from the fire itself. In our school years we had an hour or two's homework to do every night; that certainly wasn't easy, what with the poor light we had.

It was only when people went over to Scotland for work that signs of improvement could be seen for the first time in houses around the country, for they couldn't fail to notice the houses abroad, and the money they brought back helped them improve their own houses. The first improvements were made during the time the Congested Districts Board was active. One of its members, Monsignor James Walker, the parish priest at the time, was constantly urging the people to improve their houses. They should do this, they should do that, he'd say, and many took his advice. Lots of houses were given a new look, and those who improved their houses in some sort of way were given a subsidy by the board.

By the time the monsignor left for another parish in 1909, there can hardly have been a single house in the parish where the cattle and the people were covered by the same roof. Before that few people had a byre or a barn, and the cattle were kept at the lower end of the house. At the turn of the century new barns and byres were built a bit apart from the dwelling house, so there wasn't the same danger to health as before, for fever had been widespread. Build new dwelling houses, the people were told; use your old one as a byre or barn.

Another important advance too concerned the men who were working in the coal mines or shale mines in Scotland; they learned how to use powder and explosives so they knew this helped them break up rocks into stones for house-building; that also provided rubble for the roads here in Ireland.

Even in my early years there was nowhere near as much tea drunk as there is today. Tea was a novelty for us; I still remember we had tea after our supper of mashed potatoes only two times in the year – Hallowe'en night and on the eve of St Brigid's Day, 1 February. And the great improvement in clothes and footwear is amazing too. It was shawls the women all wore to mass. You would hardly see a coat on a Sunday, apart from the coats of the schoolmistresses. Children hadn't any shoes, and because we went on our bare feet, we often had bruises, chilblains and chapped feet. Children today haven't a clue about things like that.

Thanks be to God for all the changes that have taken place since the likes of me was a child.

BETWEEN TWO COUNTRIES

Having spent seven seasons in the Lagan each one straight after the other, I didn't want to go back there again. I had now spent the winter at home, and when May came round, my thoughts again turned to Scotland. One gets tired of every kind of work, and that's how I felt about the Lagan. I had made up my mind it was Scotland and nowhere else for me; I simply had to go across and find out for myself what sort of a country it was.

You can be sure I was kept busy each and every day from the day I arrived back from the Lagan. From the start of that winter all of us – my mother, my stepsister Nancy, Máire and myself – were constantly at work, knitting stockings for 'the man in Glenties'. And then, in the springtime, when the Búistéir, my stepfather, began digging ridges in the fields, we had to go out and give him a hand. With a pair of donkeys we brought up creels of seaweed and wrack from the shore; and with the donkeys and panniers we brought manure from the midden and spread it on the ridges; and after that it was time for us to set the potatoes. Nancy, Máire and myself cut the seed potatoes and dropped them in the ridges. We helped cut and load seaweed for the potato ridges on the boat, and before we left for Scotland early in June we footed and ricked the turf.

Máire had already been across a year or two; this was the first of my many trips to Scotland. We were told the pay was much better there, and even if the work was hard, the people who had worked there told us the workers in Scotland had much more time off.

In those years in Scotland before my marriage I worked at the potatoes all of time. I knew lots about housework, but I knew even more about the potato work, so I stuck to it entirely. I wasn't the only one to do that: most of the young ones went across for the potato work only, and it's the same today. I'd say between four and five hundred young boys and girls left Arranmore Island every year when I was growing up. And it wasn't only from Donegal they went – they went from other parts of Ireland as well, especially from County Mayo, from Achill, Tourmakeady, Belmullet, Gweesala, Duhoma, and so on.

Many companies specialise in the potato trade; they buy the crop and supply shops in Scotland and England. Among these companies or purchasers were The Scottish Co-Operative Society, Galbraith & Roy, Fulton & Co., Paul & Weir, Haggart & Co., and many more. These companies had offices in the towns to direct all the work, but we had little contact with them. As far as I know our bosses or gaffers would go to the offices at the start of each week to sort out any difficulties or problems.

In May agents from these companies would go to a farmer and one of them would purchase the potato crop just as it was at that time and it only half ripe, still growing. He knew the acreage of the field and it didn't take him long to reckon how much it would yield when the crop was ripe. An acre ought to yield about twelve tons of potatoes, but some soil wouldn't yield

The Firth of Forth and the bridges spanning it from Queensferry on the south to Fifeshire on the north. Many Irish workers found employment in this area long ago – tattie-hoking, farming, house-building in the towns, factories.

that amount; and again, there were other fields where the soil could produce maybe as much as fifteen tons! Frequently these buyers went back to the same farmer year after year so it was easy for them to estimate their business exactly over the whole year.

'Gaffers' is what we called the stewards who organised the potato work itself; the same name's still there today. The gaffers were Irish; most of them came from our own county or from County Mayo. Every potato company had its own gaffer, and he was the man who marked out each day's work for us from the start of the season in June until it ended round about Halloween. In the month of April the gaffers would arrive in Ireland, and visit houses in Donegal and Mayo to hire groups of people for the work two months later. Sometimes people

*The Broomielaw in Glasgow, destination point for the Irish on the
Derry Boat or the Dublin Boat.*

from the same family worked under the same gaffer year after
year. Some tattie-hokers who weren't happy with their gaffer,
would leave and hire themselves out to a different man.

The gaffer was responsible for his own band of workers.
The entire group – the men, women and children working for
the same gaffer – was called a 'squad'. All squads were paid the
same amount of money, but some gaffers were more generous,
more understanding, more thoughtful than others. Generally
these gaffers worked for the same buyer throughout their life;
in some cases when a gaffer died or grew too old for the work,
his son would be chosen in his place.

During my years in Scotland most of the gaffers came from
the western part of Connacht. I can still name many of them:
Pat Kilbane, Anthony Munnelly, Anthony Gielty, John Gielty,
Anthony Mailey, and so on. Most of their squads came from
their own county, but if they couldn't get enough workers in

Mayo, they'd come here to Donegal and sign up some more. At that time there were some buyers who had no more than a couple of gaffers, but the large companies had as many as six. The first time I went to work at the potatoes, our buyer was a Mr Burns. Our gaffer was Seán Ward from Arranmore; we knew him as Seán Taig. His mother, Bidí Róisín, was the woman who as a girl had worked along with Caitlín Bán at the kelp many years before that on Rinnanean in Iniskerragh. Seán Taig's wife, Máire, was the daughter of Dan Boyle – the master in my years at school. Seán Taig was a decent gaffer; he always did his best for us.

Normally, the year's digging started in Ayrshire, and when the digging was finished there, the squads moved on further north – Lanarkshire, Fifeshire, the Lothians, Dumbartonshire, and areas even further away – as far, maybe, as Perthshire. Ayrshire is close to the sea; it doesn't have as much frost as other areas so the crop ripens earlier there; Wigtownshire and Ayrshire were always the best places for early potatoes.

As I've said already, the gaffers would turn up in April and they'd agree a deal with the workers for the coming season; each gaffer knew who was in his squad before it was time for them to head off. The Ayrshire crop usually ripened at the beginning of June, and the squads had to be there to open it up. Sometimes, instead of just one person in the household going across, two, three, four or five might leave, and they'd all stay in the same squad throughout the season. Sisters would help their brothers – they'd wash and cook for them, and so on. At that time a young potato worker could save upwards of twenty pounds in a season, so a family with five working would save round about a hundred pounds.

On my first journey to Scotland I travelled by boat from

Arran Roads. We knew it as the Westport boat, and she'd call in at Calf Island three or four times every summer for passengers bound for Scotland. She'd leave Westport on a Saturday and arrive off the coast of Donegal on Sunday. In June she'd always anchor at Calf Island to pick up the potato workers; she'd arrive there by mid-day after mass.

I remember clearly the first day I went to Scotland. Two days earlier Seán Taig dropped into the house to tell us to be ready after mass on Sunday; he'd got word the boat would be calling some time that day. Burns & Laird, the shipping company, usually sent half a dozen posters to the island a week in advance; these posters were put up in the post office and in shops on the island to let us know the day and the time the Scottish boat would call.

Getting ready for our departure meant two really busy days for both of us – and for my mother of course. She had tons of things to do – washing, sewing, knitting, packing and so on. My mother was good at that: she had often helped us get ready for the Lagan or for Scotland. Máire and myself were big grown girls at this stage, but from the way my mother went on about everything we'd need, you'd think we were still only children.

Leaving the chapel after mass we could see the boat coming east along the old channel by Glen Head. We raced home immediately. Our mother had the dinner ready and as soon as we had eaten it, it was time to go. The steamer now had dropped anchor off Calf Island, and we saw the boats pulling out from the shore with their passengers. In no time at all we were down at Pollawaddy ourselves and one of the small boats brought us out. *Lily* was the name of the steamer; I was amazed at the size of her.

The sailors helped us climb the rope ladder they let down to us. I remember the ticket to Glasgow cost four shillings, but children paid only half fare. When the last passengers were aboard, the ladder hanging over the side was pulled up, the anchor was raised and we were on our way. Only two squads left Arranmore that day, so just about a hundred passengers in all boarded the *Lily* at Calf Island. There were upwards of thirty in each squad and some forty men travelled across as well: they were bound for work on the farms.

After we left Arran Roads we called into Kincasslagh Bay to pick up people there. We couldn't berth at the quay, for the new quay at Gortnasade wasn't built yet. After we took aboard the mainland people from Gweedore and the Rosses, we headed for the Sound of Tory and the coast at Cloughaneely. We called first at Ballyness Bay, and then went on to the Downings. What with the people who had embarked at Westport and Ballina and those that boarded the ship on the coast of Donegal there was a great crowd of us on our way to Glasgow.

Most of the westerners on board were prattling away 'as Gaeilge', the same as we were, but at the start we could hardly understand a word they were saying, for their dialect was different from ours. We were lonely leaving home, but the loneliness left us when we couldn't see our house any longer. But as soon as the loneliness disappeared, another torment took its place – seasickness. The sea wasn't rough at all, but we'd gone off in a hurry after our dinner, and since many of us had never been on a big ship before, the seasickness hit us as soon as we rounded Rosguill. I remember I threw up a couple of times; after that I felt a lot better. You could buy tea and sandwiches on the ship, but I'd been seasick a short while before and I hadn't any appetite. I drank some water, and that was all I had until we arrived in Glasgow next morning.

We hadn't a berth for the night, so we had little sleep in the course of the voyage. I was cold and I was tired from lack of food and sleep, but there was damn all we could do about that. We threw ourselves down on the deck, fixed our bundle of clothes under our head and tried to snatch a few minutes sleep. It was very, very difficult to sleep in a place like that; lots of things made it impossible: homesickness, seasickness, the racket of the engines, the rolling of the ship, things like that. I slept an hour or two, and that was it.

In the morning we were happy to be told we were on the inner side of the Mull of Kintyre and it wouldn't be long now until we'd be docking in Glasgow. The old hands told us this, and they were sure to know for most of them had spent their lives going across and back. It was nice to gaze on the sights as we approached the mouth of the Clyde. At the same time you must bear in mind that we weren't passengers going off on holiday for a week or two; we had other things on our mind beside the pretty sights; we had plenty to worry about when we thought of the work facing us between now and Hallowe'en. All the same, everything we saw was a great novelty – we had never been across to Scotland before.

Before we arrived in Glasgow the ship had to unload cattle at Greenock and again at White Inch. That held us up, but at last we reached our destination, the place known as Broomielaw. How often I had heard the old people talking about that place! And now, here was I, seeing it for myself. At this stage we were advised to keep close together, for like myself there were some in our group who had never set foot in Glasgow before. Each of us took our bundle and followed the gaffer's directions. We first had a hurried mouthful to eat, and after that we were to go to the station and take the train for Girvan.

That train left St Enoch's Station, and, if my memory serves me right, the ticket to Girvan cost only half a crown. We were tired when we arrived there later that day. I felt we had been a very long time on the go since leaving home at dinnertime the day before. Bad as that was for us, wasn't it far, far worse for the Mayo people? We had to spend only one night on that boat – those who had embarked at Westport at mid-day on Saturday and the Achill people had two nights at sea.

Some of the Connacht workers travelled as far as Girvan with us, but others went to their own destinations – Ayr, Ardrossan, Kilmarnock, Wigtown and other places. And the Arranmore men who had travelled with us on the boat and weren't bound for the potato fields went off here and there – the Lothians, Perthshire, Kelso, Galashiels and other places where they'd find the work they had come for.

After the train pulled into Girvan, we had a two-mile walk out as far as Girvan Mains, a great centre for potatoes along the seashore to the north of the town. I well remember where we were to work for the next six weeks – Jamestown Farm. The gaffer gave me the name and address for I wanted to send a note to my mother in a day or two.

As soon as we arrived at the farm, we were shown the bothy we'd be living in. There were thirty all told in the squad, sixteen women and young girls and fourteen men and boys. The men had their own bothy, and the two bothies were more or less the same size. We weren't long getting to bed that night, for the gaffer had told us we'd have to be up very early in the morning; in any case we were exhausted after the journey from Ireland.

WORKING AT THE POTATOES
IN SCOTLAND

As I've mentioned before, the potato work started in Ayrshire early in June or by the middle of the month. The new potatoes were still only half ripe, but that didn't matter: they were in great demand and fetched a high price. So the squads had to be in Scotland round about the tenth day of the month for the 'green sale' or 'green hoke' – the word they often used for it.

I'd say there are more potatoes grown in Ayrshire than in any other shire in Scotland. The Ayrshire farms are large and devil a crop of any other kind would you find there – it was all potatoes. I didn't see much wheat, oats or barley sown there, but there were several farms that kept milking cows, so they had to grow grass and kale or turnips as fodder for the winter.

The fields in Girvan Mains were huge and there was no knowing how many tons of potatoes were dug out of them. There were about thirty workers in each squad, and often as many as four squads would be working in the same field, each squad having its own stretch of work, and working apart from the other squads. Because of that the squads hadn't much contact out in the fields, but they did meet on Saturdays or Sundays, often on their way to mass, or sometimes at dances in the bothies; as well as that they met on the way into the town on Saturdays. They all got to know each other, and, in very many cases, the liking or the love lasted the rest of their life.

Men and women from Donegal and Mayo often married through working at the potatoes long ago, and because of that you'll come across Donegal husbands in the west in County Mayo and vice versa. Among the Connacht surnames to be found here in Donegal are the likes of Gannons, Henrys, Lavelles, Costellos, Howards, O'Malleys and others; in the same way you'll find Donegal names in Achill and elsewhere throughout Mayo. Lots of those marriages, as I said, stemmed from the friendship between the two counties in the potato work long ago.

Working at the potatoes is still tough, but there's no comparison with the way it was in my time over in Scotland. Today there's the electric light; we had nothing like that. Most of the time all we had when we were getting up in the morning and going to bed at night was the light of a candle. In every farm today there are tractors, lorries, mechanical diggers and every sort of appliance, each one better than the one before; there was absolutely nothing like that in our time. Most of the digging was done with graips, and the potatoes had to be lifted or gathered by hand into baskets. Usually the boys and girls did the lifting. There were three grades of potato: *ware* i.e. eating potatoes, *seed* potatoes and *broc*. These were all brought to a man with a riddle (sieve); he selected the best. There were two men standing beside him waiting until their basket was full; they'd empty them into the barrels on the field and when the barrel was full, they'd lift it up onto the cart.

The work in the potato field was as well organised as could be. Fifteen diggers – boys and girls – would dig with the

A scene familiar to the potato workers long ago – Girvan and the Ayrshire coast, and, some distance out to sea, Ailsa Craig; just visible on the horizon is the Mull of Kintyre. The trees are bent by the south-west wind the same as trees on Ireland's western coastline.

graips, and fifteen others would come after them lifting the potatoes. The diggers usually were the strongest in the squad, and the weakest ones gathered the potatoes into the baskets. The diggers usually dug two drills at a time; that meant less walking for them and the gatherers, and the work could then be done more quickly. At the same time, there's no denying that that work was terribly sore not only on the diggers but also on the boys and girls keeping up with them as they worked.

The diggers always had a leader, and the other diggers had to keep up with him throughout the day. He was called the 'fore-one', and he usually was a good worker who'd never tire from morning until night. No other digger was allowed to get ahead of the leader during the day, even if he felt like doing so. It was the usual thing for the leader to be paid a penny extra an hour to attract him to this part of the work. He enjoyed the authority this gave him and he liked being looked up to by the rest of the squad. Indeed this man often went on to become a gaffer with his own squad later on in life.

Besides the squad who did the digging and the gathering there were half a dozen other men whose job was emptying the baskets into the barrels. As the squad went to work in the morning, you'd see lots of barrels standing out there in the fields. A barrel held twelve stone of potatoes and the buyer's name was written clearly on each of them so that everyone knew who owned them. During the day carts came to the field, and when the barrels were loaded on them, they were taken to the railway station in Girvan or Portpatrick or Largs or the station nearest the squads. The train carried the potatoes to Glasgow, where a proper grading was carried out, and after that they were put in bags and despatched all over the country. Handling the baskets and the barrels was heavy work and no one would be fit for it unless he was really strong. This kind of work would never be given to a 'greenhorn' – anyway, he wouldn't be fit for it.

I'd say we had to work fifty hours per week, and the diggers and gatherers at that time were paid only three pence an hour. Before the second great war the diggers and the gatherers got six pence per hour, and the men who emptied the baskets and loaded the barrels onto the carts and lorries got one pound ten shillings a week. Our wages were only half of that.

The gaffer had to make sure the potatoes reached the train in time, so the squads had to be at work very early in the day. Since the mornings start to come later after 24 June, St John's

Argyle Street, Glasgow 1910.

Feast Day, we usually didn't start at the exact same time every morning; it was the gaffers, however, who wanted to make as early a start as possible. When we arrived early in June, we used to start at four in the morning, and we worked until two or three in the afternoon. There were many mornings we tried our best to get our breakfast ready by candlelight. At nine o'clock we stopped for a bowl of tea, and we ate our dinner usually between twelve and one. After dinner it was back again to the field for another hour or two. We didn't work on Sundays and on Saturdays we stopped at noon.

Our gaffer, Seán Ward, was really good to Máire and me; in fact he put her in charge of the housework. The person responsible for that job worked inside the bothy only. She'd have to get up very early and light the fire so that the other members of the squad would be able to make their breakfast before they started the day's work. She'd fill the kettles and put them on the fire and get the gaffer's breakfast ready. As soon as they had eaten, the whole squad would head out to the field. Máire stayed in the bothy and did the housework on her own. She'd make the beds, tidy the house, scrub the floor, take out the ashes, get a good fire going, fill the kettles a second time, and would have them boiling for the squad when they came in for their nine o'clock tea. There was more of the same to be done between then and the afternoon. She prepared all the gaffer's meals, washed his clothes, even cleaned and polished his boots for Sundays or for a trip to town if he felt like going there for the afternoon. By the same token, there weren't many gaffers that didn't go into the town when they had finished their work for the day.

We often had to stop working because the weather was too bad. If it was teeming rain, we'd come indoors, but if the rain wasn't too heavy, the gaffer would ask us to keep at it until we'd finished the day's work. Wet clothes were a big problem – we just hadn't a good system of drying them overnight. That's what the Achill men were doing at Kirkintilloch in 1947 when the bothy went up in flames. Drying clothes round the fire is extremely dangerous; and on top of that there's a risk someone might develop a bad bout of influenza from wearing clothes that weren't completely dry.

There were times on a hot summer's day when a maddening thirst would hit us. Someone would go to the bothy for a can of water; with a light shake of meal on it there was nothing better for slaking your drought.

The gaffer stayed throughout the day, but I don't think I ever saw the buyer himself in the field. Travellers from the buyers or the companies would visit the farm twice a day, in the morning after we had started, and before quitting in the afternoon. The gaffer kept a notebook; throughout the day he'd make notes in it. He also had a man working for him at the railway station; he'd check the number of wagons the gaffer despatched and write down all the details.

As I've said already, the season started in Ayrshire, and as soon as the crop there was dug out, the diggers moved somewhere else. We worked in many parts of Scotland: Lanarkshire, Renfrewshire, the Lothians, Fifeshire and Perthshire. Somehow, Ayrshire was the place that appealed to me more than anywhere else; we were close to the sea and that reminded us of home; we often went down to the shore on Sundays or in the afternoon after work, and gathered dulse, barnacles or periwinkles, the same as at home long ago.

Maidens was a fishing village, and as long as we were working in that part of the country, we were able to get fresh fish from the boatmen in the harbour. It was a really beautiful place, especially in summertime. Away to the west we could see the Antrim hills, and northwards lay the Mull of Kintyre and the mountains of Scotland. Out off the Ayrshire coast stands the great rock called Ailsa Craig or 'Paddy's Milestone', the name we usually called it by. Beyond it were all kind of ships, sailing up and down to Glasgow and Ardrossan; but, again, that brought the Derry boat to mind and thoughts of our voyage back home in November when the potato season would be over for another year. That's the distinctive thing about the Irishman; when he's in another country, he's always keeping his home in his head no matter how mean or how grand that home might be.

One thing struck me very strongly – the Scottish farmers at all times were simply great at their work; that was their livelihood, they ran their farms as efficiently and profitably as possible. They often reminded me of the farmers in the Lagan, but that's no wonder, for hadn't the forbears of the Lagan farmers come from Scotland in the first place? They shared the same basic qualities: industry, shrewdness and thriftiness, qualities they still have today.

Just the same as us back home, the Ayrshire farmers used seaweed for manure. On days when broad seaweed or wrack of any sort was washed ashore they carted it to the fields to manure the soil with it. They did this in the autumn; when they spread it on the field they ploughed it into the soil when the wrack rotted. They were people who did their best to make sure nothing ever went to waste. In summer or early in autumn they often grew kale in a field where the potatoes had all been dug out; this would provide them with fodder for the milking cows over the winter. Often their way of working was an eye-opener to us. My husband Séimí spent his whole life – from May to Christmas every year – working for a farmer near Edinburgh, and he said that every year university students came to that farm to learn all about running a farm. The hired workers, the men from Ireland, were amazed at that – imagine, people with a university education studying farming!

At that time the head of the house would often take his children – the girls as well as the boys – across for the potato season. That kept the family together, and the money earned that way was a great help in rearing the children. By spring money was always scarce, and from then right up to August goods had to be obtained on credit. By August the money would start arriving from the potato workers, and by that time too the home-grown potatoes, the early ones, were now nearly ripe and that would see an end to the hard times until St Patrick's Day came round again.

That spell – from St Patrick's Day to August – was the most miserable time of the year for the Rosses people. There wasn't much fishing in those months, and most of the money the workers brought home from Scotland the previous November was gone, and there wasn't a penny to be got anywhere else. A family here and there might get money from America, but that didn't amount to much. Expensive things had to be bought in spring: seed potatoes or corn seed, turf to be cut, and other work to be done. Often a load of seaweed had to be bought, or guano from the shop. And that was the time too when clothes might have to be bought for first communion or confirmation. No wonder money was scarce by the end of spring, and it went on being scarce right up to August.

In spite of all that it would be wrong to think the skies above us were always black and gloomy during our seasons of hard work in Scotland. No, we had the light of faith with us at all times, and it was a great support all through our lives. We were young too and that was a great help, and we were fit for a life like that, such as it was. We were all neighbours in the squad; that too made life better. When one of us received a letter from home, everyone wanted to hear whatever news was in it. We talked away in Irish all the time we were away, and really there wasn't a great deal of difference between our life across in Scotland and the life we led at home during the winter.

Nearly every squad had a fiddler or someone who could play the melodeon, and they'd be busy playing for us in the afternoon after our day's work was over, and again they'd play at the weekend. We often had dancing in our bothy, and other bothies would come in and join us; and we'd dance in their bothies too, and they'd have the same sort of crack as us. We mostly danced the old-style dances: the Sets and the Lancers, the Maggie Piggy, the Donkey, the Mazurka, the Barn Dance, those sorts of dances and more. We often made a stab at the Scottish dances as well: the Gay Gordons, the Highland, the Corn Rigs and others besides. A lot of the time there was singing; there was singing in the bothy at night and there was singing at the dances of course. These dances gave a lift to our spirits and took away our depression in the land of the stranger.

We had to cook for ourselves every day, and we brought bowls, plates, mugs, saucepans, pans and items like that with us from home. We had working clothes too, and we usually carried all these things in a big wooden trunk – kitchen-ware, working clothes, top boots for the fields, and so on. Carts would collect these trunks from the boat at the quay in Glasgow, so we didn't have to think about them until we arrived in the bothy at Girvan. The gaffer saw to it that the wooden trunks were brought to St Enoch's Station and put on the Girvan train. Beds and everything else were provided in the bothy, and we had no worries about that either. There was coal for the fire, and we were given our fill of potatoes free of charge, and very often milk could be got free from the farmhouse. We would buy groceries in the town on Saturdays, and sometimes during the week as well. We had no bother getting working clothes in the large towns – places such as Glasgow, Edinburgh, Lanark, Kilmarnock, Cupar and so on; and during the season hawkers sold us clothes in the bothy now and again.

We were very green and ignorant in our first year in Scotland, but after a season there, we got to know the country and met lots and lots of people. I must say the Scottish people were always really good to us and helped us every way they could.

But in autumn, when the Feast of the Assumption came round, we always started thinking of home. At that stage the nights were growing long and the weather was turning cold; no wonder we yearned to be back home again. The work was now wearisome, and there were nights after we'd said the rosary and were lying in our beds, a woman in the next bed might say with a sigh or a groan: 'Wouldn't it be lovely to be home right now!' There was no escaping the homesickness. It was the time of the year too when we started putting things together for the journey back to the 'auld sod'. We had to buy presents for young and old, for our own families, and we couldn't overlook our neighbours either. Often you'd promise a poor wee child a doll, maybe, as a present; promises like that have to be kept. You'd be in hot water if you arrived home empty-handed!

When I was growing up the old people lived in awful poverty. There was no pension, and they had no income of any sort. I think I must have been married a year or two before the Old Age Pension Act came in. Before that you could say there was hardly a man or a woman of advanced years who had as much as a penny for tobacco or snuff, for shoes or for clothes, and often they went about in rags; no one paid any heed to them, or showed them the slightest respect. They were moved on from son to daughter, and eventually, when the children grew tired of them, they were packed off to the workhouse in Glenties, and were never seen out again. Thank God, the old are respected and well looked after nowadays – so different from the way it was in my young days. Thanks be to God for the great changes that have occurred over the years; and great thanks are owed as well to the man who brought in the Old Age Pension Act.

Not only did we send money home to our families during the season in the potato fields, we brought home presents in November as well. Scotland was a great place for kitting ourselves out. On a Saturday you'd see something in the shops that would suit you; and you'd be able to buy more clothes, maybe a pair of boots in Edinburgh or Glasgow, or you'd see something in Derry perhaps on your way home. When we arrived back, our box-trunk would be loaded with our old working clothes, the cooking utensils and other things, but there'd be room in there for the gifts and the presents as well.

After our long hard season at the potatoes we'd be overjoyed now that we were ready for the journey back home. And naturally we were delighted to be home again, for everyone, young and old alike, had a hearty welcome for us.

THE DERRY BOAT

For several years before I married I crossed over and back to Scotland for the potato work, but after that I never returned. My husband Séimí used go across every year and I had to stay and look after things at home. Our life didn't change much when we were across there working at the potatoes. The grind got no easier, and we were getting tired of the work facing us year after year with few changes of any sort. I began to turn against Scotland and the tattie-hoking, and said to myself I'd go back to the Lagan for another year or two.

These ideas were flitting through my mind when I was working with the squad in Dumbartonshire. November was drawing near and soon the year's work would be over and the squad would be heading home for the winter. We had spent seven or eight weeks in Dumbartonshire and were beginning to get ready for the journey back. But that wasn't my plan. I'd made up my mind to go to Strabane for another year's work: wouldn't that be better than going home and spending the time making the long walk up and down to Glenties that I had been doing before this? I told nobody in the squad what I was going to do; I had it all planned out. I knew the hiring fair would be held in Strabane on Old Samhain, 12 November, so I left the squad a week before that to be back here in time. I took the ferry from Helensburgh to Greenock, and boarded the Derry boat there that evening; I remember I only had to pay six pence on the ferry. As well as taking me across, they had to transport my box-trunk as well, for I left none of my belongings behind in the bothy. There was to be no return for me.

As is often the way in November there was an angry, bristly appearance about the evening as I waited in Greenock for the Derry boat to arrive down from Glasgow. She arrived at seven o'clock, but I had to wait another two hours before she sailed. A certain amount of cargo had to be loaded, and as well as that a train from Glasgow arrived with some fifty passengers bound for Derry. Most of them were Irish; they had missed the boat in Glasgow, and came down on the train to Greenock to make sure of getting aboard. It was a Burns & Laird steamer, and I knew plenty about ships of that line for I'd often travelled on them over to Scotland and back. Some of the Burns & Laird ships would go on west to Sligo and Westport, but at this time of year the ship went direct to Derry. This ship was the *Magpie*. The Burns & Laird Company had many other ships: the *Lily*, the *Tiger*, the *Briar*, the *Lairdsloch*, and the *Pointer*. They carried cattle as well as passengers when sailing from Ireland, but at any rate, there'd be no cattle aboard on the return journey.

Seeing I was in Greenock so early, I had a chance to go about the shops and buy what I needed. One of the pieces was a nice small jacket that was in the fashion at the time. It cost twelve shillings. That's not much in today's money, but the truth is I had to work a whole week to earn twelve shillings in those days.

It was about eight o'clock when I went aboard, but the ship didn't leave for another hour. My ticket from Greenock

A view of Derry harbour at the beginning of the century.

to Derry cost four shillings, exactly the same as I used to pay years earlier on the Westport boat from Calf Island. By now I was about twenty-five, and it was high time for me to be more careful than ever with my money. I had reached a good marrying age, and I had decided it was time to save the odd pound for myself. Whatever I had earned so far kept me in clothes and footwear, and what was left over I gave to my mother. I had now saved twenty half sovereigns, and I intended keeping it for myself and adding as much as I could to it in the years ahead. The money was all gold coin, for that's the way they paid us back then. To keep my money safe I made a small purse or pocket of white cotton on the inside of my petticoat. I put the half sovereigns in it, but made sure to have enough loose change in my pockets for my fare as far as

Strabane. Above all else I didn't want to go home; if I did, my people would be expecting a large share of the money I had saved; it wouldn't be easy keeping it from them.

It was night by the time we left Greenock. I knew nobody on the boat, but I began chatting with a squad of tattie-hokers who were going back home. They were talking in Irish, so I was bold enough to ask them where they came from, and they told me they were from Annagary. We were all in high spirits because we were heading home after a tough season on farms here and there in Scotland. There was such a clear difference between people going across on the Glasgow boat and the same people coming back on it. There were smiles on everyone's face now, but those faces were often downcast and showed the track of a tear on the way abroad. It was always so, from the day Colmcille left Derry, and it always will be so. It's hard for any of us to overcome our homesickness.

Having left Greenock they opened the bar and a few of the men were pretty tipsy. One of the Annagary men had a melodeon and he began to play for us as we sailed down the mouth of the Clyde. We were still in sheltered waters and the boat wasn't swaying from side to side; she was moving on steady and calm. The Annagary man kept on playing and out went a group of young ones to dance. It wasn't the first time they danced together; like ourselves they had lots of dancing in the bothies throughout the season. When the dancing was over, they were up drinking tea at the counter, but I decided to eat nothing for fear of seasickness. After the dancing, other passengers – especially the men with a drop in them – started to sing.

Some of the singers were boys and girls who had just started working between the two countries, and because of

Derry – the Diamond.

that they hadn't any songs I hadn't heard before. At some stage in our life we had heard them all: *The Flower of Sweet Strabane, Skibbereen, My Name is Pat O'Donnell, The Maid of Culmore,* and others like them. The tea from the counter, the drink from the bar, the songs and the dancing helped us while away the early part of the night.

Then, some time around midnight, it began to get rough. People are always scared of being on the sea in rough weather, but it's a hundred times worse when you're out on the sea after nightfall. So great was our fear, we weren't able to go up on deck that night. We were dreadfully sick, and none of us was brave enough to stir from where we were sitting or lying. We hadn't a berth anyway; we were stretched out there on the floor looking the image of death. As soon as the boat left the shelter of Kintyre she started to plunge this way and that in the horrendous sea. It put the heart across us and no wonder, for this was the worst night I ever put in since I first started travelling to Scotland. I had often heard reports of the Sea of Moyle, the Moyles, but never before did I think the sea could be so vicious there. You can be sure we put in a cruel night on the high seas that night. The old-timers with us – those that had spent their life crossing over and back – even they were sick that night. We thought the night would never end until we'd reach Lough Foyle and get as far as Derry. At first we were praying, but then we grew so sick we hadn't the strength to say as much as a prayer of any sort. A woman from Cloghaneely fell against a door and blood poured from the centre of her forehead; a sailor tried to bandage her head to staunch the blood; as far as I could see he made a poor fist of it.

We ought to have been inside Lough Foyle by six in the morning, but it was ten before we gained the shelter of Inishowen, and it was after eleven by the time we docked at Derry. And now we forgot all we had come through in the hours just past; we didn't care as long as were safe on land after the battering we had suffered that night.

I was hungry now for I hadn't eaten a bite since leaving Greenock the evening before. I got a man to carry my heavy box to the station in the Waterside, and when that was dealt with, I was able to stop worrying, for looking after that box was making my head reel. I left it in the station and went off for a bowl of tea in an eating-house nearby. After that I bought my ticket for Ballymagorry, the station nearest Kitty and Patrick's home.

Ballymagorry isn't far from Strabane – the cost of the ticket, I think, is six pence. I left my box-trunk at the station, and walked out to Kitty's house. I got a great welcome there and they were delighted when I told them I was going to work another season or two on the Lagan. I stayed two nights with Kitty and her husband, Patrick McNulty, before the hiring fair on 12 November. Needless to say, Kitty and me had thousands of things to talk about. Patrick said he'd take the big box to Strabane on the hiring day, so we got up early that morning. He harnessed the horse and trap, and we didn't stop until we arrived in the town. He found a house to look after the box until the market was over. I went up to the market house where the young ones stand around waiting to be hired by the big-shots of the Lagan. It was still early in the day; the people were only starting to arrive for the fair.

Jacob Rankin of Castlederg hired me, and it's with him I spent my last two seasons in Tyrone. I made a deal that day to stay just a single half-year, but then I stayed on for another season too. This was the last Tyrone house I worked in and, more important than that, it was far and away the best house of them all. They were a pleasant, understanding couple, and there was nothing stuck up about them. Rachel, his wife, knew all about housework and farm work, and always gave me a helping hand whatever I was at. She had a nice, friendly manner, something that pleased me greatly during my time in service with her. She was a kind, gentle person, and in the morning, before I'd go out to the byre to milk the cows, she'd bring me a mug of tea and a couple of slices of bread.

Mr Rankin was a member of the Orange Order, but that made no difference. They knew I was a Catholic, but never bothered me on grounds of my religion. Above the fireplace was a large picture of King William, and they appeared to have as great a reverence for that picture as a Catholic household would have for a picture of the pope. Every day I'd be looking up at King William; no wonder every tiny feature of the king is embedded in my mind to this very day. King William wore a hat with a white band on it; he wore an embellished royal cloak; he carried a sword in his right hand and sat astride a white horse. I had tons of time too to memorise the motto at the foot of the picture:

Love God and love your brotherhood;
Honour all men and honour the King.

Not everyone in Castlederg, however, rendered obedience to King William and the Orange Order at that time. It was while I was working for Jacob Rankin I learned this humorous version of the song *An tSeanbhean Bhocht*. The title means 'the poor old woman' – she represents Ireland:

'I went one day up the bog', says the Seanbhean Bhocht.
'I went one day up the bog', says the Seanbhean Bhocht.
'I went one day up the bog and I met an Orange dog
and I skinned him like a frog,' says the Seanbhean Bhocht.

'Were you ever at Derg's fair?' says the Seanbhean Bhocht.
'Were you ever at Derg's fair?' says the Seanbhean Bhocht.
'Were you ever at Derg's fair, where they chase them here and there,
making stockings of their hair?' says the Seanbhean Bhocht.

'Were you ever in Pomeroy?' says the Seanbhean Bhocht.
'Were you ever in Pomeroy?' says the Seanbhean Bhocht.
'Were you ever in Pomeroy, where the devil jumps with joy
when he meets his Orange boys?' says the Seanbhean Bhocht.

'Were you ever in Newtownshivel?' says the Seanbhean Bhocht.
'Were you ever in Newtownshivel?' says the Seanbhean Bhocht.
'Were you ever in Newtownshivel, where the Romans chase the devil
and they make the Orange civil?' says the Seanbhean Bhocht.

I was very glad to be back in the Lagan. I knew those people already and the type of work expected of me. It was nice to be looking across at the mountains of my own county instead of the Mull of Kintyre and the Highlands of Scotland. I was older than when I came to County Tyrone long ago, and in every way I was a lot more worldly-wise. I expected to find boys and girls from the Rosses, Gweedore and Cloughaneely working round about Castlederg, and I'd have a chance to chat with them after mass on Sundays. As well as that, Castlederg's not all that far from Strabane, and maybe some day I'd be able to call on Kitty. I was happy to be working for Jacob Rankin and Rachel; they were the best people I ever came across in the Lagan.

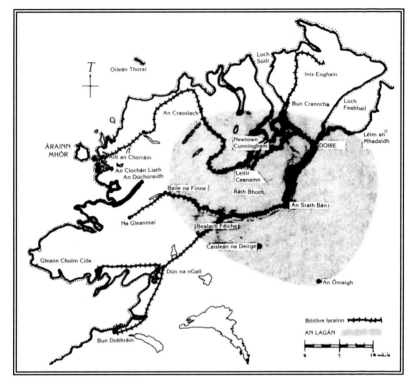

From the top:
*Oileán Thoraí – Tory Island; Loch Súilí – Lough Swilly; Inis Eoghain
– Inishowen; Loch Feabhail – Lough Foyle; Bun Cranncha – Buncrana;
An Craoslach – Creeslough; Léim an Mhadaigh – Limavady; Doire
– Derry; Newtowncunningham; Ailt an Chorráin – Burtonport; Leitir
Ceanainn – Letterkenny; An Clochán Liath – Dungloe; An Duchoraidh
– Doochary; Baile na Finne – Fintown; Ráth Bhoth – Raphoe; An Srath
Bán – Strabane; Bealach Féiche – Ballybofey; Na Gleanntaí – Glenties;
Caisleán na Deirge – Castlederg; An Ómaigh – Omagh; Dún na nGall
– Donegal Town; Gleann Cholm Cille – Glencolumbkille; Bun Dobhráin
– Bundoran.*

THE BUTCHER

His real name was Antain Gallagher, but the people always called him 'the Búistéir', for butchering, that's what he used to do in his early years. He hadn't a butcher's shop and he wasn't a journeyman butcher who travelled here and there selling meat throughout the island; no, but he was a man who knew how to do the job. If someone had a beast or a sheep they wanted killed, Antain would go to their house and carry out the butchering. My mother certainly addressed him as Antain; apart from that, as I said, he was never called anything except 'the Búistéir'.

He lived a long life. He was just one year short of the hundred when he died in 1926. Even though he was born and raised on the island, his people didn't come from Arranmore. His mother's name was Máire Boyle, but she was always called Máire Calhame, for she probably hailed from Calhame in the Annagary area. His father's name was Donncha Antain, and according to what was said locally he came into the island from Cloughaneely. In his young days, the Búistéir used to herd cattle for relations of his in that parish. Donncha Antain also lived a long life; father and son lived to the same age.

The Búistéir wasn't a big, burly man, in fact he was the very opposite – small and stout, but he was tough and wiry – and he was a first rate worker; it would be hard to find a better man at earning his keep. All through his life he turned his hand to every sort of work – farming, minding sheep, cutting seaweed or wrack in spring, fishing, making creels in the winter, and so on; he was hardly ever idle. As well as doing all those sorts of jobs here in Arranmore, he used to go across to Scotland every year for the harvest as long as God gave him the strength for it. In spite of all that hard work he lived a long life. Round the fire at night he'd say 'work never killed anybody'. Not everyone might agree with him on that, but anyway that was his opinion.

He married three times. His first wife was Maeve McGinley, daughter of Andy McGinley; she came from Leabgarrow. Early in life her eyesight began to fail, and later on the poor creature went blind. On account of Maeve's blindness the couple had a tough life. They had four children – Andy, Donncha, Máire, and another boy who died early on.

A shepherd by the name of Leitch was working for the landlord up on the hill in Arranmore at that time, and Antain used to go out and work for him. Building ditch boundaries for the landlord was what they were doing, and he often told us he was paid only a shilling a day. Nevertheless, it helped them rear the four children. Blind as she was, Maeve lived a long time. Then she fell ill and was sent away to the hospital in Glenties; not long after she was admitted she died. The family then broke up, and the Búistéir was now on his own.

The Búistéir's second wife was Peggy Connolly. The Connolly family were officially McConigley but everyone on the island called them Connolly in English. Peggy Connolly's father was Liam Connolly the husband of Anna Bhoilsigh. 'Boilseach' or 'Boilsigh' in the genitive case is a an Irish word that mean 'bulging' so Anna Bhoilsigh would probably be translated as Bulging Annie. Peggy was reared on the upper road of Leabgarrow – the ruins of the house can still be seen there. She didn't live long – she developed a leg ulcer, and that led to her death. Peggy had only one child, Nancy, and Nancy was only four years old when her mother died. Liam Connolly, the grandfather, took charge of Nancy, and he and his wife, Anna, looked after her until she was old enough to fend for herself. Later on in life Nancy married a Gweedore man, Patrick O'Donnell, and she had seven children: Maggie, Annie, Sarah, Mary, Antain, Dan and Owen. Nancy herself died in 1950 aged sixty-nine.

After the Búistéir's second marriage he built a cabin up at the top of Leabgarrow on the edge of the bog; it was as high and steep a place as you'd find on the island. He built it by the side of the road that leads out to the lighthouse; in fact the only other house between it and the lighthouse was Cowan's house; that was situated at the head of the lake between the top of the hill and the lighthouse itself. Cowan was a supervisor or land-steward; he was employed by the landlord, and he built the house up there to be close to his work.

Building that cabin on his own was hard, exhausting work for the Búistéir; it took him a long time to complete the job. He made a cosy kitchen for himself and Peggy, and he used to tell us it was thatched knee-deep in rushes. Peggy's brothers – Mickey, Condy and Seán – helped him finish the work, and by the time it was ready it had a fine, neat appearance. There was plenty wood around at the time: you'd find fir in the bog and, as well as that, planks were often washed ashore. It wasn't easy hiding those planks from the eyes of the revenue men or the police or the bailiffs, but it's likely the Búistéir had ways of getting round that.

Arranmore courthouse was built by the authorities in Dublin Castle at the behest of landlord Charley. Cases were heard there until Sinn Féin courts were established during the first Dáil.

But the story didn't end there. The Búistéir hadn't asked John Stoupe Charley's permission to build the new house and now he was in great trouble for he had broken the landlord's 'law'. According to regulations laid down by Charley, no one could build a house or a dwelling of any kind unless he first got the landlord's permission. According to landlord Charley's 'rules' in those days, building a second house on any farm in the estate was forbidden. The Búistéir had broken this so-called 'law', and he was summoned for acting contrary to the landlord. The Búistéir had been under no illusion about this from start to finish; he well knew what he was doing was forbidden, but in spite of that he went ahead and finished it.

The day of the trial arrived and the case was heard in the courthouse, the building at the Dreen (An Draighean) in Leabgarrow. At that time the hearings were held once a month, and the judge, solicitors, clerk of the court and the other officials would come in for the day from the mainland. The case was called, and after evidence from the police, from Charley and others, the verdict was returned against the Búistéir. According to the 'law' in force he was ordered to quit the mountain and raze the cabin he had built to the ground. On his way out the door with the hearing now over, the Búistéir turned round and glowering at the bench he shouted: 'Tiocfaidh an lá go fóill agus beidh an oiread céanna talaimh agam féin le Mr Charley (The day will come when I'll have as much land as Mr Charley).'

They were all amazed when they heard this outburst from the Búistéir. They were taken aback. The judge asked the Búistéir to come up to him and explain what he had shouted at the court. He wasn't a bit slow to spell it out to them.

Said he: 'Tá tréan talaimh ag Mr Charley anois agus níl dada agamsa. Ach tiocfaidh an lá go fóill a mbeimid araon cothrom. Beidh an méid céanna talaimh ag an phéire againn an lá a shínfear muid san uaigh (Mr Charley has a powerful lot of land at present and I have nothing. But there's a day coming when the two of us will be equal. On that day we'll have exactly the same amount of land – the day the two of us are stretched out in the grave).'

Everyone was dumbstruck, they could find no answer to that. But at this point the landlord himself stood up, and looking down at the Búistéir standing there beside the bench he declared that the Búistéir he could stay on where he was on the mountain, and, for better or worse, he wouldn't have to demolish his house. That's how it happened and the Búistéir lived there from then on, and it's in that house myself and my sisters were reared. In his day the Búistéir got the better of the landlord.

The Búistéir was the man of the house and a good man of the house he was. Kitty, Máire and I were reared there along with Nancy, our stepsister, and there was never a spiteful word between us. As for the Búistéir, you wouldn't find his equal from one end of the country to the other. He was always pleasant and kind to us from the very first day we arrived at his door. He and my mother were married in April 1885, and a month or so later we all came in from the mainland and went up to his house on the hill. We were happy with him as our stepfather since it wasn't God's will to leave us our own father when we were children.

The Búistéir's house was a marvellous house in those years. I'd say no woman in that part of the country could come anywhere near my mother as regards singing; and for story-telling and folklore, I'm thinking you'd never find the likes of the Búistéir anywhere in his day. The story of the Fianna and legends of every sort – he had them all. On winter nights the house was often crammed to the door with people hanging on his every word once he got going on the stories. Half of them had nothing to sit on – they'd have to squat on their hunkers with their backs against the wall. The Búistéir of course hadn't far to go for turf – there were turf banks there right behind the house – so he'd always have a roaring fire. He was a decent, friendly, welcoming man who never begrudged his hospitality to anyone no matter how many arrived in for the night's craic. He was renowned as a storyteller, a fact he himself was well aware of. He was our last great storyteller in Arranmore. His stories, I think, weren't written down, more's the pity. Some people said a priest or a schoolmaster had copied down a fair number of them; if they did, no one ever saw them in print. I'm afraid they're now gone forever.

Often people came from as far away as Aphort. Even though they had often been here before and had heard all his stories, they still came back. I can still see him there, sitting on the stool between the fire and the bed, his cap laid aside, the clay pipe in his mouth, chatting with the people who came in for the evening. Then when he had drawn his last pull on the pipe, he'd place it inside on the hob, stretch himself back on the stool and then launch into his story. He had all the stories on the tip of his tongue, never so much as a word out of place. They were exactly as he had heard them around the fire long ago from his father, Donncha Antain and his mother, Máire Calhame. It seemed to me there was a nobility, a richness in his voice as he recited the sagas of the Red Branch Knights. There was a certain magic in the words as he narrated the story of Conall Cearnach:

Teacht dheirg an dá néal maidin shamhraidh a bhí ann ins an aimsir chianaosta. Níor luaithe a chonaic Conal Cearnach ball bán ar an lá ná scairt sé ar a cheithre feara déag a bheith ina suí i bhfaitheadh na súl … Shín an rása acu fríd gleannta agus chnoca fiáine, seal go hioscadaí, seal go hascaillí i bhfraoch agus i bhfásaigh nó go raibh neoin bheag agus deireadh an lae ann, éanacha beaga na coille craobhaí ag gabháil fá fhoscadh agus dídean, an capall beag ag gabháil faoi scáth na copóige agus chopóg á diúltú fá dhídean na hoíche …

It was the first flush of dawn on a summer's morning long ago in the ancient past. The moment Conal Cearnach discerned the dawn he summoned his fourteen warriors to be up in the blink of an eye … The chase went on through glens and desolate hills, over all manner of terrain, by heather and plain till eventide had come and the long day was done, the small birds seeking shelter and cover in the branches of the forests, the horse-fly seeking the shelter of the dock leaf and the dock leaf refusing the horse-fly shelter or cover for the night …

And it was the same too when he recited the stories of the Fianna:

> In aimsir Chormaic Mhic Airt bhí an saol go haoibhinn ait, bhí naoi gcnó ar gach craobhín agus naoi gcraobhín ar gach slait (In the reign of Cormac MacArt life was enchanting; nine nuts sprouted on every twig and nine twigs grew on every branch …)

The youngsters would stay there listening to him, all thoughts of leaving for home far from their mind. And I too often sat there, listening to him reciting the cycles, but it was my mother's songs that gripped me far more than the stories the Búistéir recited. I'd always had a fancy for the music, the same as my mother long ago, singing as she went about the jobs around the house.

But the Búistéir didn't spend all his time narrating the heroic cycles. He had no end of folklore concerning events here on the island hundreds of years ago. He was about twenty in the year of the Famine, 1847, and remembered clearly the state the people were in at that time. He'd say a man would come to you in spring asking you to let him dig up the soil where there had been a crop of potatoes the previous year; he wouldn't ask for pay – all he wanted was permission to take home at the end of the day any potatoes he might find still lying there. People gathered the plant known as chickweed and boiled it into some sort of broth. Water was put in the pot as well, a bowl of oatmeal was added, and it was all cooked together for food. That sort of 'food' was difficult to stomach; it was said it sometimes brought on disease.

There were three broth or soup stations on the island at that time, and Jimmy Boyle (he was called Jimmy Condy

Dónal Ruadh) would come in from the mainland to dole
it out. Jimmy was Daniel Boyle's brother – the Daniel who
was to be our teacher later on in the island. All Condy Dónal
Ruadh's family were well educated and later in life Séamus
himself became clerk of the court. He shared out the Indian
meal at that time; the Búistéir, however, told us he gave each
house only two stone of meal; in many families they had to
make that small amount go very far.

You'll hear people suggesting the hunger wasn't as severe
in Arranmore as it was throughout the mainland for there
was plenty of sea-food there for people to lay their hands on
– dulse, sloak, carrageen, barnacles, winkles, and so on. The
sea-food wasn't really a great help; the Búistéir told us the
cargoes of meal that were brought into Rutland Harbour was
far better for the people of the Rosses throughout the Famine
time.

The broth was cooked at three places: at the top of
Leabgarrow (just down from the house Joe Johndy was
to live in later); the field next Antain O'Donnell's house in
Fallagowan; and beside the house Antain Eoin once lived in
just beside the river in Ballintra. In his day Antain Eoin was
probably a landlord's bailiff and he was the one who made the
soup at that station.

The Búistéir told us a Cloghcor man came up for the soup
one day, but before he got as far as the soup station, he dropped
dead. The Búistéir used to tell us that that's when the new
landlord, Charley, bought the island from Lord Conyngham.
Conyngham's bailiffs, the minister from Maghery, Valentine
Griffith, the island's priest Father James Hargan and the coastguards were the members of the committee which was set up
to help those in hardship or in poverty.

Father James Hargan ministered to the island during the Famine. It was another sixty years before a parochial house was to be built in the island, so during his time here Father James Hargan lodged in Fallagowan in the middle of the island. He was well on in years when he came here, and he lodged in Mickey Mhacain's house. In spite of his age he did great work for the people throughout the Famine. He'd go on foot to the houses bringing relief to people in need, and, said the Búistéir, he was often seen helping the men carry the dead down to the burial ground at Cashelnageeragh (Caiseal na gCaorach), and he helped to bury them too. He was seven years on the island when he was struck down with an illness and died. He is buried in the Cashel graveyard, the place he had helped bury the dead during the Famine.

The Búistéir lived to a great age, and saw many changes during his life. He used to say that more than a dozen priests ministered to the island in his time. In his early years Conyngham was the landlord, but as he never resided in the Rosses, everything had to be done by his agent, Foster of Roshine, Burtonport. During the Famine Charley became the new landlord, and the Búistéir saw the end of his time too. He saw the police come to their barracks at Pollawaddy and forty years later he saw them leave. In his lifetime he saw more changes than anyone else.

Up to the present day people often speak of the kind of life we led 'in the time of the English', meaning the time the landlords, the police and the coastguards ran everything in the island. It must be said that not all of them were English, but that's the label we gave them for they were upholders of English law. All during their time here they ruled the island with an iron fist; no wonder the people were delighted the day they left. It wasn't only in language they differed from us: their religion too was different. They were Protestants, and they had a small church at Leabgarrow for their service every Sunday. It was built beside 'The Big House', a couple of years before landlord Charley died. As far as religion is concerned, I can honestly say they never interfered with our beliefs in any way and we didn't interfere in theirs. There was never any friction between us on that score.

The Búistéir's father, Donncha Antain, had neither love nor affection for the 'Sasanaigh' as he called them. 'May I never depart this life,' he'd say, 'till I see the last of them gone from the island.' Years passed and the landlord's family left and now Magee was the only one still on the island – the man who had been Charley's agent. The age of the landlords was now over; Magee still ran the post office however, and he had a small shop in Leabgarrow. He was the odd one out in Arranmore; his companions were all gone; he decided to follow them. Donncha Antain was making a hurried visit down to Leabgarrow this day; he dropped into John Nancy's house – John Nancy was a relation of his. The moment he stepped in the door, the man of the house greeted him in these words: 'Donncha, God has finally granted your wish. Magee left the island this morning.'

Hearing that the old man simply took off his cap. 'Thanks be to God', he said; he had gained his request at last, and not long after that Donncha passed away.

The Búistéir had a sister by the name of Róise; she married a man from Newry, John Kelly. John was a weaver by trade, but he hadn't a loom during his time here on the island, and didn't do any weaving at all. But he was good with his hands and used to turn out tubs and churns for anybody that wanted them.

Patrick Kerr, his wife Rose, and their two children along with Róise Rua, whom they hired around 1905.

As I said earlier, the Búistéir's first wife was Maeve, the daughter of Andy McGinley. In his day Andy was a great man for telling traditional tales and the people of the surrounding area often gathered in his house to pass the night listening to him. He wasn't great at the old cycles – he acknowledged the Búistéir as his master in that field – but he had all sorts of folklore – the prophecies of Colmcille and lots more.

MY WEDDING DAY

My husband's name is Séamas MacGrianna, or Séimí MacGrianna as he was known. We had known each other from when we were children for he was a neighbour of ours. He was a son of Donny Sheáin MacGrianna and his wife Nuala and they lived at Screig an tSeabhaic – a townland only two hundred yards from where I was reared. They came from the Annagary district on the mainland, Nuala from Braade and Donny from Diarach, but they made their home in Arranmore after their marriage. People referred to her as Nuala Mór in her time; her surname was Duffy, a fairly common name around Annagary. Donny Sheáin had been married before, but his first wife died when she was young. He had one child from that marriage – a son named Seán. Donny and Nuala Mór had six children – Hugh, Michael, Paddy, Séamí, Bríd and Eveline.

I had reached a good marrying age by this time – twenty-nine; my husband was a couple of years younger than me. As I mentioned before, I put no money by for myself until I was old enough to plan for the future. I managed to save a little sum of money by this time; it wasn't what could be called a lot of money, but even so it was a tidy amount at the time. It was hard to build up savings, for we weren't paid much, and as well as buying footwear and clothes for myself and the others, it was very, very hard to stop handing money over to my mother.

We were married here on the island on 21 January 1908. Fr Dominick Canning was stationed here. I didn't know much about the priests for I was home only part of the year and couldn't get to know them really well. Fr Eamonn Doherty I knew much better – he was here before Fr Canning. Fr Eamonn came from Fanad; his Irish was good; he was interested in music as well, and often came up to our house. My mother would sing for him; he took down the words of the songs, and as far as I know he published some of them later on. He was the man who built the parochial house; before that the priest hadn't a house on the island. He left Ireland later on and spent the rest of his life with the Maynooth Mission in China. He was a priest who served God as diligently as he could.

Another couple were married the same day as Séamí and me – Michael Ward from Fallagowan and Bríd Molloy from Ploghogue. We knew her as Biddy Chaithlín; she was the daughter of Dominick Molloy and Caitlín Bhán. I mentioned Caitlín Bhán already; she was the one who cajoled the thread-man in Glenties long ago, when she was making the long walk with the 'queen's stockings', and I also mentioned the lament she composed the day she lost the kelp across at Rinnanean. Throughout my time on the island there was nobody who could match her at storytelling and that's a fact; she was outstanding too at the sacred poetry; you couldn't ask for anything more pleasing than to hear her reciting those poems. She'd go to wakes as far over as Aphort; not only did she give out the prayers – she'd go on and sing the sacred songs as well: songs such as *Dán an Toir*, *Dán an Bháis*, *Dán na hAoine* and so on. She died in 1944; she wasn't that old – not much past the pension age.

Neighbours of ours – Joseph and Mary Boyle – were our best man and bridesmaid. After we left the chapel, we all walked up as far as the bridge in Ballintra. Michael Ward and Biddy Chaithlín's group turned off to the west, and we went east towards the village. We were to have a party in Johnny Hiúdán's at Leabgarrow, and the other group were to meet at Hiúdaí Ruaidh's, not far from their own place. There were upwards of twenty in the two groups.

I still remember my wedding day very clearly and the hard frost there was as we made our way to the village. We made our way on foot – there was no transport on the island in those days. When we were going eastwards along the Dreen (An Draighean) and down the Schoolhouse Brae, the ground was so slippery we couldn't walk in the middle of the road but had to keep to the grass verge next to the ditch. When we arrived at the pub we were delighted to find a roaring fire laid on for us.

All the men in the party went down to the bar for a drink and the women sat round the fire in the kitchen. That was the custom in those days; it wasn't the done thing for women to stand at the bar counter in the company of men. After they had a drink for themselves, a couple of them came up and asked us what we'd like to drink. Seeing the day was cold everyone had a half measure of whiskey, and the woman of the house helped us make punch. After we'd had another couple of drinks the woman of the house gave us all a bowl of tea. She offered tea to the men too, but they didn't take her up on her offer – they probably preferred to stick to what they were drinking.

Phil Néill Neansaí Boyle and his wife, Sarah. They died in a railway accident near Creeslough in 1925. Phil, an accomplished fiddler, supplied the music at Róise's wedding feast in January 1908.

After a couple of drinks the men weren't content to stay down in the bar; they came up to us, and for the rest of the day they moved between the bar and the kitchen. After an hour or so one of them went out in the middle of the floor to dance on his own. There was no fiddler in the party, so he gave me the job of lilting for him. I had learned the mouth-music from my mother, for, God rest her, there was no woman on the island who could lilt like her. I had done a great deal of lilting myself. It was a reel he wanted, so I did my best to lilt *Ruball na Fáinleoige (The Swallows Tail)*.

After another couple of drinks, they insisted that nothing would please them better than to hear a song from me. I laughed at that and I told them someone else would have to do the singing instead of me: wasn't it my wedding day – it wouldn't do for me to be singing at my own wedding party. But there was no arguing with them; they one and all declared I was the best, and sure wasn't it only natural I should have a good voice for wasn't I the daughter of Maighréad Ward 'the best woman to sing there ever was on the island'. There was no getting out of it – I had to sing a couple of songs to please them. Since we were in Johnny Húdán's – 'the wee house at the side of the road' – the man of the house asked me to sing them the song Peadar Breathnach composed long ago about Nóra Hiúdáin. I sang it, and Johnny was very grateful. After that I sang *An Spealadóir (The Scytheman)* and *Na Francaigh Bhána (The White Frenchmen)*. By now it was past dinner-time, and we felt we should be heading for home. We were to have our wedding feast up at the Búistéir's, and as we got near the house, we could see they'd a great fire blazing for us. My mother shook me by the hand and kissed me. The Búistéir did the very same, the two of them wishing us a very happy marriage.

Our dinner was ready for us. The Búistéir had killed a sheep, so we weren't short of food for the occasion, and we weren't short of drink either for whiskey was cheap – only four shillings a bottle; holding a feast in those days didn't cost a lot. Later on in came Phil Néill Neansaí Boyle, the fiddler, and he kept us in music until well into the morning. Phil lived in Leabgarrow, and in those years he was in great demand at wedding parties all over the island. We had a great time throughout the night, for as well as the dancing we had songs and stories. Not a being left the house until one hour after daybreak – plainly, everyone there was satisfied and more than satisfied.

After we were married, Séamí built a small house close to his father's and it's there we've lived ever since. It wasn't

Séimí and Róise towards the end of their lives, summer 1954, outside their house.

big, but it was big enough for the pair of us since we never had any children. Donny Sheáin had about five acres of land and he gave half of it to Séimí and me. Marriage made very little difference to the sort of life I'd been living up to then: I hadn't to go far from home, and I had the same friends I grew up with. I was glad to be near home, and could visit my mother and the Búistéir whenever I pleased. My mother lived until 1920; she was eighty-six when God called her. The Búistéir lived another six years; he died just one year short of the hundred. God rest the two of them.

Family tree:
Seán Hiúdaí Ward (Cruit) = (1) Máire Coll of Cruit; she died
    young and (2) Máire O'Donnell.

This was Máire O'Donnell's second marriage. She had previously married Manus Gallagher who drowned in Arran Roads and had two children by him. To survive widow O'Donnell married widower Seán Hiúdaí Ward and they had three daughters, Róise, Bríd and Maighréad.

Maighréad who was Róise Rua's mother married Thomas Coll and they had five children, Kitty born 1874, Máire born 1876 and Róise Rua born 1879. Two other children, Donnchadh and Nuala died in infancy – croup.

Donncha Rua Coll the Poitín maker had nine sons and one of them Thomas married Maighréad Ward. Thomas died in Glenties hospital in 1883.

1885 Maighréad married Antain Ó Gallchóir, the Búistéir; died 1920 aged eighty-six, died 1926 aged ninety-nine.

Kitty Coll married Patrick McNulty,

Róise Coll married Séimí MacGrianna 21 January 1908. They had no children.

The Búistéir married three times:

(1) Maeve McGinley – went blind – died Glenties. Four children – quartered out. The Búistéir couldn't look after four children; Maeve's relatives cared for them.

(2) Peggy Connolly (or more correctly McConigley but that family were called Connolly on the island) – one child Neansaí. Had seven children with Patrick O'Donnell a man from Gweedore, died 1950. Again, widow marrying widower to avoid death in the poorhouse.

(3) Maighréad Coll – with her three remaining children – Kitty, Máire, Róise. Widow Maighréad couldn't rear three children without help; married the Búistéir.

THE IRISHMEN AT WORK
IN SCOTLAND

The Donegal people always knew a great deal about Scotland. Not only did they know the cities and the large towns – they knew in detail tiny districts throughout the country as well. There weren't many parts of the country they hadn't been in sometime in their life: the Orkneys, the Hebrides, the Isle of Sky, the Highlands, the Lothians and the south of the country down as far as the Cheviots. Few counties in Ireland apart possibly from Mayo had as close a connection with the Scots as Donegal and its people.

Long ago the two main topics the men of Arranmore talked about as they sat around the fire at night were fishing and the work in Scotland. They described the places they had been, the great schemes they had worked on, the people from all quarters they had met, and more on the same lines. It was easy to keep on at that: everyone knew what lay behind the other person's story and everyone knew the places they were talking about. It gave married couples lots to talk about too, for it wasn't the husband only who was an authority on Scotland – most of the women had spent their young years there too and understood everything their husband would mention when he arrived back home.

Séimí, my husband, crossed over and back to Scotland

when he was a boy, and he went on doing that till he was too old for it. That was how his father Doney Sheáin had spent his life, and every year he brought Séimí and his other sons across with him when they were big enough; his own father Seán MacGrianna had done the exact same in his day. That was their inheritance, the routine they were reared to, and nobody ever heard a word of complaint from them.

We only had little patches of land, scraps of soil that would never deserve the name 'farm', but we did see really great farms in our time, those in the Lagan in the early years of our work and the farms in Scotland later on. The farms in Scotland were massive, and it's still the same today. They tell me the farms close to the large towns and cities have changed, but there aren't as many changes further out in the country. As far as crops are concerned and the ways they are farmed there have been changes, some big, some small, but the fields, the hawthorn fences and the farmhouses are there still. New farmhouses may have been built here and there, and extensions added to other farmhouses, but, by and large, there has been little change. And that applies as well to the farms we worked on in County Tyrone.

I learned a fair amount about farming during my time in the Lagan and also in the tattie-hoking squads here and there in Scotland in the years before my marriage. And the neighbours who'd drop into the house for the chat – Eoghan Ned MacGrianna, Seánín Johnny Mór Ua Cnáimhsí, Phil John Neansaí – they'd go on and on about the work in Scotland. They often discussed Jack Hermesson's huge farm just outside Edinburgh, a hundred acres of the best land in Scotland, a farm that employed Irishmen all year round. He had ten ploughmen and ten Irishmen, and he took on more

Irishmen in the spring and autumn. He kept twenty-five horses and a pair of horses was assigned to each ploughman for the ploughing in winter and at the start of spring.

On large Scottish farms the owner didn't issue the orders personally – he had men to do that for him. These were the foreman and the man next in rank – the grieve. The farmer, as far as I know, outlined the work to be done and these two men saw to it that everything was properly carried out. The foreman passed the orders to the grieve, and he in turn told the ploughmen and the other workers what they had to do.

Some Irishmen did every sort of work: coal-mining, navvy-ing, laying sewer pipes, brick-laying in the big towns, and so on. Some of them even spent the season in the fisheries, or on trawlers fishing out of Aberdeen, Fraserburgh, Peterhead, and other ports like them. But that wasn't my husband's way; he spent all his life at the farmwork, and not only that – he spent most of his time on just one farm, Robert Love's, at Ballarno outside Edinburgh. His father Doney Sheáin MacGrianna had worked on that farm too, and it was Doney who took Séimí and his other sons there in the first place. They knew this farmer well and they knew the locality and the kind of work expected of them and they never moved far from it. From then on throughout their life Love's farm in Ballarno was like a home to them.

Séimí would leave for Scotland in mid-May and he'd be away until Christmas. Some of the men with him would stay on until the following St Patrick's Day, but my husband preferred to return before Christmas. I was on my own at home, and I didn't want to be on my own as much as a day after Christmas.

Robert Love's farm wasn't as big as Jack Hermesson's – the

Edinburgh Castle, and below it the Grassmarket, a major hiring point for spailpíns, mowers, and other farm workers.

one I mentioned a few moments ago. Robert Love had just five ploughmen and five Irishmen. As well as these men, he'd employ other Irishmen for the harvest. Among the Irish he employed through the year were Séimí and his brothers Paddy and Hughie; two of the Colls from Aphort, Hugh and Eamonn Rua; and one of the Boyles from Leabgarrow, Johnny Joe Johndy. Another Boyle from the mainland worked on the next farm, Johnny Johndy from Clogherdillure near Burtonport. At night and at weekends he often dropped into the bothy at Love's.

When they went across in mid-May they worked at the turnips. By now the turnips tops were showing and they had to hoe and grub them. The potato stalks too would be showing and they had to weed and hoe them in the same way and prepare them for moulding later on. It was the ploughman and his team of horses of course that did the actual moulding. The Irishmen were paid every week; at the beginning of the century they were paid only one pound, but wages rose sharply in Scotland and England during the First World War. Even so, they were still paid only two pound a week at the outbreak of the Second World War. They were given extra if they had to work late in the evening or on Saturdays; they'd get perhaps two pounds and ten shillings or two pound and fifteen shillings, or even as much as three pounds.

After hoeing and weeding the turnips in the middle of May they next had to thin or 'single' them as they used call it. Séimí and the other Irish workers were all expected to give a helping hand, but sometimes workers were specially recruited for the job. Those men weren't paid by the day but by the piece; in the old way of reckoning the customary rate for thinning a hundred yards was one and a half, two or two and a half pence.

After the potato and turnip drills were tidied, the haymaking started in June. The owners of the large farms used huge, strong Clydesdales for ploughing and every other sort of work; these horses pulled the reapers that cut the hay and the corn. Séimí and his squad had to clear a space at the head of the field for the machine to turn around; this space was called the head-rig, and they cleared it with scythes. When the hay was cut, they had to help turn and dry it and then stack it in lumps or large cocks.

After the hay was saved, it was time to start cutting the grain crops – oats, barley, rye or wheat. Away back, when Séimí's father used go across, the Irish cut a large amount of the corn on the Scottish farms with their own hooks or sickles. They brought their sickles across with them, and took them home again at the end of the season. But the mechanical reapers had arrived by Séimí's time. He and the others had to lift the corn behind the machine and gather it in sheaves. They put eight sheaves in a stook and stood them up in such a way as each side of the stook got the same amount of sunshine. Later, they built the sheaves in stacks in the stackyard or haggard and put a thatch on them to keep them dry throughout the winter.

They didn't have to work along with the squads of potato-gatherers in the late summer and autumn, but if it happened the farmer wanted potatoes for his own use, they had to help store them in a pit. In winter, when every other kind of work was over, they had to thresh the corn and transport the grain to the local granary. Before despatching the grain to the mill to be ground into meal, they turned it with shovels. Throughout the year lots of different sorts of jobs were done as well. Some men were more skilful with their hands than their fellow-workers, and the Irish labourers wouldn't be long there till the foreman or the grieve would be aware of that. If there wasn't much work for them in the fields, he'd have them doing this and that around the farm – trimming hedges, whitewashing the byre, mending spouts, twisting straw ropes for keeping the thatches secure on the hay stacks and corn stacks in autumn, and so on; the grieve never left them idle for long.

At that time Scottish farmers felt it was very important to keep livestock and the same holds true today. Some farms kept between a hundred and a hundred and fifty bullocks over winter and sold them the following summer. They seldom kept them through the summer. Many of these bullocks were of Irish stock. During the winter when these sturdy animals were housed in the byre, they were fed great amounts of hay, so when spring came there was no shortage of manure. The Irish workers had to spread it on the soil; as well as putting it on tillage they put it on grassland to improve the growth for the new season.

Love had a herd of ninety milch cows and the milk was sold every day to a dairy in Edinburgh. The cows were milked twice a day, at nine in the morning and in the afternoon at four. These animals were left out overnight during the summer, but at the beginning of November they were brought inside. The women on the farm, the wives of the ploughmen, and the men all helped with the cattle and the milking. Those cows were as dear to them as our own children would be to us here in Ireland. They even had names for them – Jean, Molly, Betty, and so on. The milkmaids were always dressed in white. The Irishmen used to help clean out the byres and, as I said earlier, they whitewashed the byres as well.

The Irishmen had a house on the farm they usually called

a bothy, but their bothy wasn't the same as the big ones the squad of tattie-hokers lived in. Bothies in fact varied from farm to farm. Often in the old times cattle were turned out of the shed they had been housed in over the winter, and it was then fixed up as a bothy for the Irish. The bothy on Love's farm was quite comfortable. It was a four-roomed house and it did the six of them very well. It had a good fireplace too, and they always kept a good fire going for they got the coal free. Milk and potatoes were free too. They'd buy food in the town on Saturdays and during the week a van came round to the bothy from the shop.

The farmer supplied their bedclothes, so they had no hardship at all. They had an old gramophone at first, but at last they got a small radio. Nobody ever interfered with them. On Saturdays the foreman would come to the bothy with their week's pay. They were happy with that. Among themselves they always talked in Irish, but they used English when they were talking to anyone else; and every night before they went to bed they recited the rosary the same as at home.

Séimí took a trip into Edinburgh every Saturday. He used to visit people from Arranmore who lived there and later in the afternoon he'd go round the shops in the city. He'd have a couple of pints before heading back to the bothy. He rarely went on his own, usually he went with one of the others in the bothy. I'd advised him not to go about on his own in the land of the stranger, and he took my advice. Every Sunday they went to mass in Edinburgh, for the nearest Catholic church was in the city. They'd meet hundreds of people from home there and there was always a great warm welcome for them. They'd get all the news about Ireland and Scotland before going back to the bothy.

Séimí told me they hardly ever left the bothy after returning from mass. Apart from haymaking and harvesting the corn in autumn – rare exceptions indeed – the Scottish farmers did no work on the Sabbath; they honoured the commandment faithfully, observed Sunday as a day of rest.

That's not to say the men in the bothy had the whole day free. There were lots of jobs to do they couldn't fit in during the week. There was cooking to be done, utensils to be cleaned, the floor to be brushed, the bothy to be cleaned and tidied up and so on. Each of them had his own washing to do and his clothes might need to be repaired – maybe a patch on the trousers, a button to be sowed on. Their working clothes naturally had to be washed frequently.

Letters had to be written home and this was always done on Sundays. Most of them hadn't been burdened by much education, so they were a bit tardy about using the pen. As for my husband, I have to admit he was never able to write anything; he had to depend on a neighbour to do that for him once a week or maybe once a fortnight. He had been to school only three days in his life! So, even though I used to write to Séimí every fortnight all the time he was abroad, he could neither read nor answer my letters. It was Seán Boyle – Johnny Joe Johndy – his workmate throughout those years who wrote the letters for him.

I thank God sincerely I hadn't the same disadvantage. I had a small bit of learning, enough to serve my purpose in any case. I must thank my mother, for she kept me at school, and I owe my thanks to Master Boyle for all he did for me during my time at school; he made every effort to help us. Because of that I was able to fend for myself when it came to reading and writing after I left school. I was able to write a short letter to my mother when I was working on the Lagan, and I kept on doing that throughout my years in Scotland. It's a bit difficult to write now for the eyesight's not great, but I can still read a little. My neighbours often bring me books and papers, and I read them here by the fireside at night, the *Derry Journal*, the *Far East*, *Africa*, *The Irish Messenger* and *Ireland's Own*. These help pass the night, and reading them is easier now that we've got the electric light.

At home we spoke Gaeilge all the time; the only English we learned was what we got every day at school. I learned a certain amount of English long ago when I was growing up, and that English was a help to me when I had to leave for County Tyrone. My English was fairly good by the time I went to Scotland. I'm glad of that, for I don't know what I would have done without it when I headed off as a child to work among strangers.

Around the fire long ago many stories were told about the misery of the destitute Irish emigrants – particularly those without any English as they struggled to make a living in Scotland or America. The Búistéir often talked about a man by the name of Seán Conaghan. It seems he had come in from the mainland and settled in the island sometime before the year of the Famine. After the Famine huge numbers crossed to Scotland every year in the hope of getting two months work at the harvest. A group of men, say ten or twelve of them, would go across towards the end of the summer and they'd all stay together till they came back home again. Seán Conaghan would head off for the harvest along with the others. He could never be described as suitable for that sort of work – he hadn't grown up with it from his early years like the other men, but they were delighted to have him in the group for his English was good and that's just what they needed – someone able to talk to farmers, foremen, lodging-house keepers and so on. In that way Seán Conaghan had the edge on the other men in Arranmore.

WORKING AT HOME

Year after year Séimí went across in the middle of May and didn't come home until just before Christmas; all that time I was left on my own. That's the way it was for the women of the Rosses a long time back – a tough existence. Bad though it was for women like me, it was a hundred times worse for those who had children. The father would be away for maybe as much as nine months in a year, and bringing up the children was a great burden for the mother. Often the father seemed a stranger – there's no surprise in that, for the children only saw him a couple of months each year. He'd write home regularly all the time he was away, but even so, that didn't banish the loneliness that's part and parcel of migration. Séimí too would write every fortnight and send me the money, but all the same there was a long, painful wait every year. He never returned empty-handed – he'd always have a present of some sort. Sometimes he'd buy it in Edinburgh, sometimes in Glasgow, maybe in Derry on the way home.

From time to time you'll hear people criticising Scotland, but nobody in Arranmore will say anything against that country; there was always employment for us there; without the money from Scotland we'd never have been able to survive.

Séimí wasn't idle long when he was back home; he soon found something that had to be looked after. He'd repair the byre and barn, feed the cow and the donkey every day, and leave enough hay in the corner to tide them over the night. When they had to be kept indoors on a rainy day, he'd fetch buckets of water from the well behind the house. He'd make a bedding of rushes in the byre, and every fortnight without fail he'd tidy up the midden. He'd clean out the byre every other day, and now and again he'd add turf mould to the midden as well.

Year after year we harvested round about a ton of hay and two smallish stacks of corn. Those stacks wouldn't be threshed until Séimí came home, and he'd thresh one of them the first day right for the job. He used the flail; the two wooden parts – the staff and the beater – would last a lifetime, but every three or four years the thong had to be replaced. It was hard, exhausting work. He'd start early in the morning so as to have the bulk of it done by nightfall. In the afternoon I'd often go out to the barn and help bag the corn. Long ago we used to take the bags to the mill in Dungloe where they'd grind it into meal, but it's ages since the last time we did that. When he'd finished the threshing, Séimí would break out the sheaves on the floor and make up 'battles' or bundles of the straw; that was the winter's fodder for the cow and the donkey.

And a day or two after Christmas Day he'd open the potato pit and turn them. Any that were rotten he'd get rid of, and he'd nip the buds off any that were sprouting; he'd close up the pit again and cover the potatoes with the same sods and scraws they had used when the ridges were dug out in the autumn.

About thirty years ago Séimí became eligible for the dole; it was 1934 – the year the dole first came in. A week before he returned home I'd write to the employment exchange in Dungloe for an application form. On the weeks he wasn't working he'd complete that form and the following Monday he'd receive the dole. Gangs of men were sometimes employed in public works on the main roads, and he was often asked to report for work. This work always cropped up in the middle of winter, and often the weather was so bad they couldn't get much done for their pay. And very often too they were working on the hill, making roads through the bogs and mending side roads. It seemed to me that the winter with its dark days was the wrong time for that sort of work; later in the year would be far better – there'd be a stretch in the day and the weather would be more kindly.

During the winter there were other things Séimí was busy at as well: he made creels or baskets for anyone that wanted them. There were lots of sally rods on the island and his customers brought him as many as he'd need. There was a green tummock in the middle of the barn and that's where he did the work. He'd work in there from nine in the morning until the light faded, and by then he'd have finished the creel. When he first started this, he charged three shillings; it rose to five and then ten; I think a creel costs fifteen shillings today. Any time in the winter you can buy them at the fair in Dungloe.

He used to make three types of creel – shoulder creels, donkey creels and panniers. The panniers were loaded with manure from the midden, and then it was brought out to the grass fields and the fields that were being tilled. The bottom of the pannier was much broader than the mouth, and when you released the hinge on the base, it emptied easily. Whoever led the donkey or pony pulled the bar that kept the hinge closed; the hinge opened, the manure fell on the ground, the hinge was closed with the same bar, and back they'd go for another load.

People needed panniers for drawing loads on their donkeys; Séimí wove panniers from a big sheaf of straw. When the pannier was made, the customer – the man who supplied the straw – would collect it at our house. It would be strapped to the breeching, the belly-band and the straddle, and the donkey was now fully harnessed.

He usually worked at the creels and the panniers on cold, wet, wintry days when he hadn't the heart to work out of doors. At the end of the winter he'd spend a couple of days opening trenches to make the soil nice and dry for delving early in spring. There wasn't even one horse and plough team on Arranmore; year after year the delving had to be done by spade – brutal work, and the men often got cramps in their wrists and arms during the first days' delving. That harsh work wasn't needed in a field where there was corn or potatoes the year before; fallow land, however, was rock hard. Séimí dug up the small garden beside the house as well as the fields a bit farther away; he usually set a hundred, maybe two hundred slips of kale and he'd sow a smallish drill of carrots as well. I tended the garden myself when he was away in Scotland. He'd spend a day or two mending ditches, gaps and fences to keep the cow from getting out of our fields – and to keep other people's sheep from getting in! As I said, there was always something to be done.

Our land wasn't good, and there wasn't much of it – about three acres all told. It was rough, hilly ground, and for the most part the soil was no deeper than the spade. It was boggy too in places, for turf had been cut around us in the past, and the cut-away bog had been worked over again and again to make it arable. The Búistéir's farm was even further up the hill, and poor as our soil was, his was worse for he was there on

Róise Rua and her next-door neighbour, Brigid Greene on their way home after rickling or footing the turf on the mountain.

the edge of the bog. The Búistéir used to burn the land every March or April after delving it in February. At that time of the year there was usually a dry spell or it might be blustery, and the people took advantage of those conditions to fire the land. They collected lumps of roughage they called stumps, pieces of bog fir and so on and set fire to them. These fires burned for a week or so, and the ashes were then raked into the soil and the field dug up once again.

You could only do this sort of burning in moorland or bog-land. The Búistéir used to tell us how he lost an entire field one night long ago. It was spring and it's likely he had burned the field the previous week. By now the stumps should have burned out and it would be time to start the raking. That night, however, a fierce gale blew up – the ashes were swept all over the place. Tilling that 'field' was a total waste of time.

Séimí used to set the potatoes every year at the end of March or early April. He liked to have them all set by mid-April, and then he would sow the corn. Down to the shore he'd go and cut a load of seaweed for the potato ridges; that kept him busy for a week or a fortnight. He'd spread sea wrack on the kale garden too and some on turnip drills. Our soil wasn't rich; if you didn't put lots and lots of manure into it, you got absolutely nothing out of it.

When he had finished all that farming work, he'd start cutting the turf; one of the neighbours would help him and every year they'd swap days. We usually had the turf cut and footed before Séimí went to Scotland in the middle of May, and, as I said, I was on my own from then to Christmas. Year after year, that was our life.

And how did I spend my time while my husband was away from home? Like Séimí I was never idle long and that's the truth. Ricking or footing the turf and roofing or covering it against the rain was only one of many jobs. Over the summer I'd draw the turf home with the donkey. Every day I brought two pannier loads until at last I'd have the whole lot home. I'd draw one load before dinner-time and the other in the afternoon. There were things to be done round the house after that, and I'd let the donkey out in the field where she could graze and get a rest. As the turf stack at the side of the house grew bigger, I'd top it with sods.

With the turf all home it was time for the hay, and a neighbour would do a day's mowing for me. The neighbours would be back again to help me stack it in the middle of August when it was dry. After that, I'd cut the grass on the ditches with the sickle, and when it was dry, I'd store it in the barn for the cow and the donkey. By now the corn was ripe. I prided myself on my skill with the reaping-hook; I never needed anyone to cut the corn for me. The neighbours, however, helped me build the stacks, and that was the end of it apart from thatching the stacks with rushes to keep the corn dry; that wasn't difficult – the stacks were small and low, but my neighbours would give me a hand at that too.

At harvest time I'd often do the cutting for others who were short of help. A woman's husband might be away in Scotland and I'd cut it for her. It was hard work – bending down cutting corn all day long is very sore on the back. It had to be gathered into sheaves as well and then sheaves stood up in stooks. The usual rate for that work was just two shillings or half a crown a day, but you got your meals as well.

And now it was time for the potatoes. I was well able for that no matter how much we had planted. A neighbour would come and build a pit to store them in over the winter. The stack-garden or haggard was the safest place for the pit; there was a fence around it to keep any donkeys from getting in and kicking the pit open; in wintertime donkeys often strayed, grass and everything else was scarce. In spring, before he'd leave for Scotland, Séimí would cut scraws – big heavy top sods from the bog; he'd bring them down to the garden and they'd be there for us when we closed over the potato pit some months later in the year.

When he was reciting the Fenian cycle, the Búistéir would tell us that Fionn MacCool and the Fianna long ago used to divide the year in two; it was the same with Séimí and me – half the year together, the other half here on my own. Summer was a lonely time; no wonder I was anxious for Christmas when he'd be back for another while.

Farm labourers didn't earn much in Scotland in those years – just about two pounds a week up to the 1939 war. The navvies were paid between eight and ten pounds, but Séimí didn't do that sort of work. Every fortnight he'd post me the money and I did my best to save as much as I could. I had a savings book in the post office and, if I could manage it, I'd lodge a pound or two. There were times, though, when bedclothes had to be bought or maybe I needed some clothes; things had to be got for the house too, so a month might go by and I'd have nothing to put in the book. Séimí hardly ever bought a suit or any other clothes here in Ireland, but he had plenty with him when he came back from Scotland. He was never sore on new clothes; a Sunday suit would last him five or six years – he only wore it once a week.

Needless to say people found it hard to save money. From when we grew up Séimí and me toiled and toiled, and at the end of day we've little to show for it all. We always kept a cow and a dozen hens or so and that was a great help for we hardly ever had to buy milk or eggs. We've no cow now – we sold her ten years ago; it was obvious we were getting too old to look after her. Today it's mostly tinned milk or condensed milk that I buy – you won't get any other kind in Arranmore, especially throughout the winter.

Séimí was never short of milk when he was working in Scotland – during the year the workers in the bothy were given it free from the farmhouse. So we missed the cow greatly when we sold her. He felt we should keep her another year or two, but I nagged him and did what I could to put him off the notion: if we were to keep the cow, the man of the house would have to keep tilling the fields – a cow has to be fed well if she's to produce any milk. As soon as Séimí qualified for the pension, I urged him to sell her straightaway, for he was now too old to be labouring with the spade. On top of that, when you're looking after a cow there's work to be done all through the year: she has to be taken out to the field and taken in again; she has to be milked and fed; she needs a bedding of rushes, and so on. We realised we were getting too old for all that. There was nothing else for it – we just had to sell her. It wasn't easy parting with her, but it couldn't be helped. I still keep half a dozen hens; some of the neighbours tell me to get rid of them too; I haven't taken their advice – so far.

As I said, we hadn't put much money aside by the time we got the pension. We had no children to bring us home some money; we only had whatever we had earned in our lifetime. But there's no point in worrying about money now; God gave us enough to get on with, and it's certain He won't let us down in the end of our days.

As for fishing, Séimí didn't spend much time at it after he married though he had fished long ago with his father, Doney Sheáin. The herring season lasted through the winter – from November to St Brigid's Day – and it was in full swing by the time Séimí arrived back from Scotland. In any case he would have found it hard to get a place on the boats. But he could always be relied on to stand in for somebody else if one of the crew was sick or something like that; that, however, didn't happen very often. In spring he'd spend a while fishing ballan wrasse or pollock, something for the dinner. He always knew how to earn some money; if there was a bob to be made, he'd have a go at it.

OUR LIVES DURING THE WAR

It was my lot to live through two great wars. Food was scarce during the first war, so mutton, beef, eggs and every other kind of food fetched a good price throughout the conflict. Because fishing on the coasts of Scotland and England was limited then, there was a great demand for all kinds of fish, and the fishermen of the Rosses and, indeed, fishermen all round this coast worked hard to earn as much as they could. Before the outbreak of war a cran of herring was sold for as little as a pound or two, but when the scarcity came, the price climbed to nine pounds. That was thought a great price at that time, but it must be borne in mind that the price of everything else went up too. Before the war a herring net cost just two pounds; nowadays the same net would cost as much as thirteen pounds.

During the war there was plenty of work to be got all over Scotland; at that time the Rosses people didn't go as far as England or Wales, but they were to do so later on; Scotland was where they all went. Since the war was being waged at sea as well as on the mainland of Europe, ships were being sunk every day, ships that were carrying food and munitions to England. Because of that the British government set about producing more food at home to feed the population – it was a busy time for the Scottish farmers. Right through the war Séimí and his brothers worked on Robert Love's farm at Ballarno, and earned a great deal of money there.

With all that work in Scotland, labourers were better paid. With a huge number of Scottish workers joining the forces, it was difficult to find men fit and able for a day's work. Throughout Scotland major war-schemes were under construction and the Irish workers on those schemes were paid good money.

There was lots of flotsam and jetsam during the first war and the men of the island were busy combing the shore early and late, hoping to come across something valuable. Ships' boats, barrels of oil, timber, stuff like that were often cast up in those years and were a rich prize for the finders. Unbeknownst to the coastguards, the police and the legal authorities, these finds were sold to buyers and fetched a good price.

There was far more washed ashore during the First World War than in the last war. People said it was the aeroplanes that were responsible for that. I was told the aeroplanes kept the submarines a lot further out at sea in the Second World War, so not nearly as many ships were sunk close to the Irish coast. Most of the wreckage in the second war was carried by the tide and the wind away as far as the coasts of Scotland and Norway.

In the First World War men from Arranmore served in the British and American armies; some of them were killed in action; others died in the great flu at the end of the war. Most of those who died from the flu were working in Scotland when they came down with it. It's likely they didn't get the best of care when they fell sick; the flu attacked such huge numbers of people it wasn't easy to bring in a system that might cure them all. Whiskey was said to be the best cure, but whiskey itself was in short supply too for the war had gone on for four years. Up to a dozen Arranmore men died from the flu; in the county itself there were hundreds of deaths.

There was a gap of only twenty-one years between the two wars. As Andy McGinley said, when reciting the prophecies of long ago, each of the wars came 'between the mowing of the hay and the cutting of the corn'. As for the second war, we had been expecting it a year or so beforehand, so it actually wasn't a terrible shock when it did break out. England was already preparing for war; indeed, before the war started, lots and lots of work was available in Scotland.

I remember clearly the day the second great war started – Sunday, 3 September 1939. Early in the day it was announced on the radio that the war had begun; I hadn't a radio, so I didn't know about it until the afternoon. The corn was cut a couple of days earlier and it was time to stack it. Since I had no help then – Séimí was away in Scotland – I asked Owen Ned and Paddy Kitty, neighbours of mine, to help me build the stack. Paddy Kitty was the first to arrive and he told me the war had been going on since the morning. Owen had the same news.

A fine autumn afternoon it was; we were carrying the sheaves into the stack-garden and we weren't long doing that. Just as we were finishing, an aeroplane flew overhead – something we had rarely seen until then. It came in from the west, from Glen Head, and we kept watching it until it went out of sight heading towards Bloody Foreland and Tory Sound. As I said, we seldom saw anything like that in this part of the country; we were totally surprised.

Paddy and Owen had often seen planes in Scotland, but I myself couldn't remember seeing an aeroplane around here for ages. In fact it was seven years since I had last seen an aeroplane. It was in the month of May and the two of us – Séimí and myself – were out turning the turf on the hill. With that we noticed a buzzing noise away out to sea and the sound grew louder and louder. Before long to our amazement we saw this small object in the sky and it was gradually getting bigger. It was a small red aeroplane – the first I had ever laid eyes on in my life. It was flying so low I could make out the letters on it clearly. It went out across Arran Roads, as if heading for Dungloe or Letterkenny. Two days later the paper reported that it landed in Derry. There was only one person on the plane – Amelia Earhart – and she had just completed the long flight from America. To be able to make that journey without any sleep at night and flying completely on her own was thought a great achievement in her time.

Very soon after the outbreak of the second war Séimí wrote from Scotland telling me not to be worried about him. They were working, he said, two miles outside Edinburgh, and weren't in any danger at all. 'I hardly think they'll send us out to fight. I wasn't conscripted in the first war when I was in the prime of my life, so there's little chance the likes of me will be called up now seeing the age I am.' That's what he said – too old now, he claimed, to be sent out to fight. In any event he was sorely needed where he was; he was working flat out in the campaign to provide food for the country at a time when others were away fighting. His letter cheered me up and gave me heart; I wasn't anxious any longer.

As I say, the war started on 3 September. Next day, the first Monday of the month, was the fair day in Dungloe; I went out to it for I had things to do there. The war of course was on everyone's mind; it was the big worry. During the night the

Athenia, a huge liner, was sunk in the ocean away west of us and everyone was talking about it; she had left Glasgow outward bound for America when she was torpedoed; hundreds of passengers were killed or drowned, we were told.

The following spring – 1940 – another large ship was lost in the same area. This was the *Arandora Star* and she was bound for Canada packed with civilians – Germans and Italians resident in England; they had been imprisoned when the war broke out. Those people had shops, restaurants, those types of business throughout England and they were kept in prison camps. The English felt it would be better if they were transferred to Canada before the war in Europe started in real earnest. They were put on board the *Arandora Star* bound for Montreal. Two hundred miles west of Tory, she was sunk just like the *Athenia* six months earlier. Thousands were lost, and their corpses were washed ashore everywhere along the coast from Erris Head to Malin Head. Many corpses were found on the shores of the Rosses and Gweedore; they were buried in Templecrone; some of them were buried in Arranmore too and in Cruit, in Magheragallen and in several other places. In the same year bodies of many soldiers and sailors were also washed up on these shores.

In September 1940 'The Timber Ship' arrived off our coast. Her real name was the *Leonidas* but the only name I ever heard her called was 'The Timber Ship'. The locals said she was on her way from Canada to Glasgow with a cargo of timber, and probably struck a mine or was torpedoed somewhere far west of our county. She was first spotted a couple of miles west of Arranmore Head drifting at the mercy of the current and the wind. She was boarded, but there was no trace of the crew, living or dead. It was widely believed the sailors took to the

174 – Róise Rua

July 1947. The then Taoiseach, Eamonn de Valera, visiting the island. He is wearing homespun clothes a present he was given when he called to the Aran Islands, County Galway on his way north. With him are Father Charlie McDevitt, the curate, and schoolmaster Barney Gallagher.

lifeboats, and a warship or some other vessel picked them up. There was food on the mess table, but it wasn't eaten, so likely they had no time to do anything except get off the ship as fast as they could. The current carried her into Boylagh Bay, and there she lay for three or four days behind Iniskerragh before the tide carried her as far as Roninis.

I warrant ye, the Rosses people were not idle while that ship was lying there. They rowed out and scrambled aboard her, and carried away as much of the cargo as they could. They piled the planks on their boats, brought it home and later in the day went back for more. They should have been cutting the corn at the time, but with 'The Timber Ship' on the coast they had no interest in anything else. The arrival of a salvage tug put an end to it; the *Leonidas* was towed off to Glasgow or Belfast. A wealth of timber had been brought ashore from her; the Rosses boatmen were very disappointed to see her go.

Timber became expensive later on and scarce too and it was badly needed for improving houses or for building new ones. We got nothing from 'The Timber Ship' – Séimí was in Scotland at the time.

Aboard the *Leonidas* were two goats and a young Jersey bull. Barney MacGill, a local shopkeeper, bought the bull from the man who brought it ashore; he planned to keep it and use it to service his own herd. His cows were on a farm up near Glenties, and straightaway he let loose the young bull among them. But the story turned out badly for Barney – he was summoned for keeping an unlicensed bull and had to have it slaughtered by a butcher. Barney Gallagher, a local schoolteacher, composed a ballad about the event and up to a few years ago it was often sung at dances and all over the island on a night when there was a drink or two to be had at a party:

Attention pay, all countrymen
to these few lines I've penned.
My freedom and my liberty
upon you now depend.

My trials and misfortune
I'll relate to you in full
and I hope that you'll see justice done
to a poor wee Jersey bull.

I was born in far-off Canada
where prairies do abound.
And on their grassy lonesome plains
I grazed and roamed around.
Till at last my master sold me
and I had to cross the sea
and bid adieu to those grassy plains
in the land of liberty.

I was shipped aboard a timber boat,
her name was Greek to me.
To far-off Liverpool we were bound
across the angry sea.
But off the isle of Arranmore,
that little island green,
our ship it was torpedoed
by a German submarine.

The crew they all abandoned us,
I'm sorry for to say
to drift upon that sinking ship
which blew into Boylagh Bay.
But soon our plight was noticed
by some natives from the shore:
They rescued me and set me free
on the hills of Arranmore.

My comrades died of hardship
upon those barren hills.
In hunger and starvation then
I wandered to McGill's.
That kindly man he welcomed me
and fed me of the best.

Then sent me to his farm
in Glenties for to rest.

Farewell to lovely Arranmore,
its hills and valleys green.
To Ballintra and Aphort Strand
where I had so happy been.
And to McGill, that gallant man,
who like Cúchulainn bold
stood in the 'bearna bhaoil' for me
as the hero did of old.

The war went on day and night out in the Atlantic Ocean and
often the fight was only a few miles away from where we lived.
Often in summer when we were out working at the turf on the
hill, we could see a line of vessels far off on the horizon heading
for seaports in Britain with every kind of cargo from America
and Canada. Aeroplanes would fly over them, guarding them
from the submarines that were lying in wait. In those days
English and American planes were flying over the island all the
time, especially in summer when the days were long and the
weather was fine. Often in those nights when I was in bed, one
of these huge aeroplanes would fly over the house – you'd think
it was trying to keep us from sleeping! The fierce noise of the
plane would grow louder and louder until it was directly above
us, and then it would ease off as it went on east or west.

Throughout the war the Irish army maintained a look out
post (the LOP) near Arran Head and I used to talk to the
soldiers based up there. In summer I'd come across them on
my way up the hill for a load of turf. They often helped when I
was loading the creels, and they did as much as they could for
me. There were six soldiers stationed there, but only two were

on duty at a time. A small concrete hut was built for them at the head of the cliff and a telephone line ran up to it.

There was a great shortage of food during the war. It was rationed and every family had a ration book to make sure they got their share of certain groceries. Coupons were needed before you could buy butter, tea, sugar, clothes, and so on in the shops.

I found the shortage of tea the worst hardship of all. I was accustomed to drink a bowl of tea, maybe half a dozen times during the day; it was very, very hard to have to do without it during the war, for two ounces of tea a week was all anyone got. You could buy cocoa and coffee in the shops and people often drank that in place of tea, but somehow I never developed a taste for either. You can be sure our joy knew no bounds when the war came to an end and tea and every other kind of food grew plentiful once again.

Bread was scarce too during the war. The flour was produced by mixing wheat from foreign countries with a big amount of Irish grain; because of that, the bread was black compared to what we'd had before the war. Black and all as it was, we didn't refuse it, for it helped keep us alive. They had lovely white bread in Scotland and the six counties, but we seldom got any of that. It goes without saying I was the happy woman when Séimí returned at Christmas, for one of the things he'd bring home were the white loaves he bought in Derry and he usually brought a couple of pounds of tea as well. I remember the pleasure we'd have – our next-door neighbours, Neilly Ned and Eoghan, and the two of us – sitting round the fire drinking a bowl of tea and the novelty of the white bread along with it.

Oil was extremely scarce too, but that shortage somehow wasn't as bitter a torment as the shortage of tea and food. Very often I was loath to light the lamp before Christmas, for I wanted to spare the oil for Christmas and the depths of winter when I'd have Séimí at home with me again. Early in winter I'd often take my knitting needles and go for an evening's crack in a house nearby. It was lonesome to be on my own at home, and that was a far better way of passing the night. The houses I used to visit were hardly ever short of light, for most of them were fishermen's houses, and early on in winter fishermen were given a special allowance for their boat; there'd be enough light for them to repair their nets and lobster pots after dark when they weren't busy at any other sort of work. I'd rake the fire before leaving the house, and you can be sure those nights in the other houses was a great saving of turf and oil at that time of the year.

The war brought great changes in the way the workers travelled to Scotland. Before the war they went across to Glasgow on the Derry boat; that service didn't operate any more – they now had to go by Belfast and Larne. A travel permit was needed and you had to get that from Dublin through the gardaí. Séimí got a permit that was valid to the end of the war. Peadar O'Donnell was working for the Irish government throughout the war, and often helped the people of this island who were trying to go across at short notice. He had a soft spot for the people of Arranmore since his time here as a schoolteacher and all though his life the island was very dear to him.

One afternoon in May 1943 myself and Séimí were sitting outside the door, looking around, enjoying the scenery. It was a fine afternoon and the weather was lovely. We had spent the day footing turf – no wonder we were tired. We had drunk a bowl of tea and were having a rest. Suddenly there was a huge explosion east of us as if it came from Kincasslagh or Annagary or Gweedore.

The island's lifeboat – powered by sails and oars.

'That's surely a ship east at Tory,' I said. 'Some poor creatures must have died this very instant?'

Séimí only made the sign of the cross and shook his head. We thought no more about it that night, but next day the postman brought us the news: the previous afternoon a huge mine was washed ashore at Ballymanus in the Annagary district. It exploded and nineteen young lads from the area were killed. This incident was called the Ballymanus disaster. God between us and all harm! Such an awful cross for a place like that.

During the war people would search the bay for any wrack or flotsam and often they brought a corpse ashore in the afternoon. They'd send word of this to the gardaí in Burtonport, and gardaí would come in and bury the corpse; the local coastguards often helped too. Sometimes the corpse

Arranmore lifeboat in the late 1930s.

could be identified by means of letters or cards, but frequently there wouldn't even be as much as that to indicate where the corpse had come from. One of my neighbours, Paddy Jack O'Hara, was a busy forager in his day; he often came across a corpse floating somewhere down the bay. One of them was the corpse of a woman, and from what he told us afterwards she was as stylishly dressed a woman as he had ever seen. She was wearing a beautiful silk dress, he said, and a fur coat as well. That was early in the summer of 1940 and Paddy believed she was one of the passengers on the *Arandora Star* that had been sunk a day or two before.

Besides those whose bodies were recovered, huge numbers were lost without trace. But there were some who with God's help managed to survive in spite of the danger. One of these was a young man from Liverpool who came ashore not far from us after a day or two on a raft. He was on a British cargo ship that left Sligo for Glasgow but was sunk in Tory Sound. Out of a crew of eight or nine he was the only one to survive. Fishermen from Pollawaddy saw the raft coming up the bay and they went out in a small boat and rescued him. No wonder he was grateful to them, for without doubt he would have perished if the raft was swept on another bit further for he'd be facing steep cliffs and rocks that nobody could get clear of. He's been living in Liverpool since then, and I think he never went back to sea. Every year without fail, he sends Christmas cards to the people that rescued him more than fifteen years ago.

As far back as I can remember and further back than that there's been a lifeboat here in Arranmore. She was often called out, night or day, to help a boat or a ship in danger anywhere between Erris Head and Malin Head or even further away than that. The crew were extremely busy during the war. They earned great respect for their work on a Dutch vessel, the *Stolwyk* that went on the rocks on a small island near Inisbofin Island on 7 December 1940. At 6.30 a.m. on that morning the Arranmore lifeboat set out. The weather that day was horrendous with mad north-westerly gales. The ship had been part of a convoy travelling from America to Britain when she suffered damage to her rudder and drifted towards the shore near Inisbofin Island. A British navy escort vessel had put down a rowing boat in an attempt to place a towline aboard the *Stolwyk*. The sea overcame that rowing boat and the four men in it were lost. Ten men from the *Stolwyk* then tried to row away from the stricken ship in one of *Stolwyk*'s lifeboats. The wind and sea drove them back smashing their lifeboat against the hull of the ship. They drowned as well. When the Arranmore lifeboat arrived at the ship it was then on a reef near Inisbofin with eighteen men on board huddled in stern end of the ship. The lifeboat reached the vessel at one o'clock, anchored and re-anchored a few times as the anchor was not gripping on the seabed. When securely anchored the lifeboat fired a breeches buoy line to the ship. The *Stolwyk* crew then dragged the line with a rope block at its end to the ship. The block with an endless rope running through fixed to the lifeboat was then fixed to the ship and the breeches buoy hauled to the ship by means of the endless rope. A sailor then stepped into the breeches buoy as he would step into a pair of breeches and that is how it gets it name. He was then dragged suspended in mid air back to the lifeboat. One by one the crew were being taken off in this manner. On two occasions the rope snapped as it had weakened from chaffing against the side of the ship and on each occasion a very frightened sailor in the breeches buoy fell into the water. He was then dragged through the water to the lifeboat. There was an anxious moment when the line broke for the second time and the lifeboat prepared to fire the line gun again. There were four cartridges left and as the lifeboat crewman prepared to fire it became apparent that seawater and rain had wet the cartridges. The next three cartridges failed to fire and there was then only one cartridge left. Even if it fired the line might not follow it because it had not been boxed or packed correctly in the factory or because the wind was too strong and the line was being fired into the wind. If the line did not reach the ship

Personnel of the Arranmore lifeboat, who rescued the crew of eighteen from the Stolwyk, *December 1940.*
Standing: from left, Johnny Bán Byrne (Johnny was not with the lifeboat crew on the Stolwyk *'run' but his two sons Phil and Neilly were) Leabgarrow, his son, Phil Byrne, Leabgarrow; Tadhg Ward, Ballintra and Neilly Byrne, Leabgarrow.*
Seated: from left, Brian (Nellie) Gallagher; Paddy Chondy O'Donnell; Jack (Charlie) Boyle; Joe (Annie) Rodgers and Phil (Charlie) Boyle all from Leabgarrow.

for whatever reason there was no way of taking the last three men off the ship. But the last cartridge fired and the line shot across the *Stolwyk*. The block was dragged through the water and secured to the *Stolwyk*, the breeches buoy dragged to the ship and dragged back with a man in it and by repeating the exercise three times the last three men were brought to safety. It was five o'clock and the lifeboat then turned for home with twenty-five men on board. By nine o'clock the lifeboat had landed at Burtonport and the lifeboat then returned next day to Arranmore.

Jack (Charlie) Boyle Coxswain was given the RNLI gold medal, his brother Phil (Charlie) Boyle, assistant coxswain and Teague Ward mechanic were given the silver medal and the rest of the crew, brothers Phil and Neilly Byrne, Paddy (Condy) O'Donnell, Joe (Annie) Rodgers and Brian (Nellie) Gallagher were each given the bronze medal for their efforts in the rescue. Jack Charlie was also given a gold medal by the Dutch government as the *Stolwyk* had been a ship of that country. In all seven crews were honoured by the RNLI for wartime rescues and two of them were Irish, the crew of the Arranmore lifeboat and the crew of the Newcastle, County Down, lifeboat.

FOLKLORE

PEADAR BREATHNACH
IN ARRANMORE

I never knew Peadar Breathnach for he lived before my time. The Búistéir used to say that he and Peadar were of an age, so that means he was born round about 1825. He came from Glenfinn, from a place called Meenagulana in the Ballinamore district. He was a tailor, but in his early days he didn't work in the one spot only; no, he went around the country, tailoring a while here, and a while there. There were no draper's shops then and never such a thing as a ready-made suit. There were lots of sheep around, and after the sheep were shorn, the wool was spun on the wheel. I can vouch for it that every house had a spinning wheel. The thread was taken to the weaver and woven into cloth. That was the system, and after that tailors came round and made suits and other garments from the cloth.

That's the way Peadar Breathnach and the others did it. He'd spend a fortnight or longer in one area and when he'd completed his tailoring there, he'd go somewhere else. According to reports, Peadar was a journeyman tailor only in his early years. Later, he settled down in his native Ballinamore, and that's where he died and him only forty-five. That was sometime in 1870, nine years before I was born.

The Búistéir – God be good to him – often brought Peadar's name into the conversation. According to the Búistéir he was a tall, handsome man – as fine a fellow as came into the island in his time. The Búistéir claimed that Nora O'Donnell – Nora Hiúdáin – could have married Peadar, but she chose Liam Hiudie Boyle, a local man instead.

It was just before the Famine, I think, when Peadar arrived in Arranmore. According to folklore he came across Nora Hiúdáin and another girl when they were loading seaweed from the strand down at Leabgarrow. Peadar greeted them and they started to chat. Nora was the daughter of Hiúdáin, a wealthy man, the owner of one of the pubs in the island. The pub is still there, but it's another O'Donnell – Matthew – who owns it now. Nora's brother Johnny inherited the pub when his father died. Johnny had a son named Patrick and a houseful of daughters – Gráinne, Síle, Nora, Bríd, Maighréad and Isobel.

Here's how Peadar starts his story:

Chuaigh mé seal tamaill ar cuairt, gur bhreathnaigh mé uaim an spear,
thart fá na hoileáin de ruaig, mar eilit is cú ina diaidh.
Sé deireadh gach duine fán chuan, nuair a tháinig mé anuas fán chéidh,
'Ó, aithním go maith ar do ghruaim, gur fear thú a bhfuil tóir 'do dhiaidh.'

I spent some time on a visit to have a quick look round about me,
rushing about the islands like a doe with a hound on her track.
They all remarked at the harbour, the day when I stepped ashore at the pier,
'By the worried look on your face a pack is surely pursuing you.'

It's then that he meets Nora, as he informs us:

Casadh domh cailín deas óg, is má casadh, sí a labhair go gear:
'Más fear thú a bhain do mhnaoi óig, ní mholaim go mór do
  chéird.
Chonaic mé fear as tír mór, is é ag imeacht gan bhróig inné,
is é mheasaim gur tusa an fear óg, a bhfuiltear sa tóir 'na
  dhiaidh.'

I met a sweet young girl, but if I did, she spoke with a cutting
  tongue:
'If you're a lad that interferes with young women, your trade I
  despise.
Yesterday I spied a man from the mainland, barefoot he was as
  he ran,
It's my belief you must be the young fellow the pack is hotly
  pursuing.'

Peadar tells her he doesn't like her mockery and begs her to
stop it:

D'fhreagair mé an ainnir dheas óg, gur ghlac mé go mór a
  scéal:
'Stadaigí 'é mhagadh níos mó, ní duine den tsórt sin mé.
Mura ndruide sibh anall de mo chóir, is stad de bhur nglór gan
  fheidhm,
Rachaidh mé os coinne bhur srón, amach go tír mór de léim.'

I answered that lovely young girl whose words cut me sore to
  the heart:
'Leave off your mocking at once! I'm not the sort you describe.
If you don't state what is fair by me and quit your clamour this
  instant,
in front of your very nose I'll leap straight out to the mainland.'

At that the mocking stopped; he hadn't to thole any more of
her slanders!

Ó, thit muid i dtuirse is i mbrón, is d'fhiafraíos den óigbhean
    chaoin
cá bhfaighimis gloine le hól, a thógfadh an brón seo dínn?
'Tá teach beag ar leataobh an róid, is coinníonn sé i gcónaí
    braon,
gabh thusa agus rapáil an bord, is ní íocfaidh do phóca aon
    phingin.

'Twas then we grew tired and serious, and I asked this refined
    young girl
where a drink might be had that would banish this gloom
    affecting us both.
'There's a wee house by the side of the road that always keeps a
    drop,
Go up there and rap on the counter, and you won't be a penny
    the poorer.'

Peadar was delighted with the welcome he got, and, what do
you think, in a trice the place was full to the door:

Níorbh fhada a bhí mise tigh an óil, gur chruinnigh an t-aos óg
    'un tí,
gach duine is a ghloine ina dhorn, le comóradh a thabhairt don
    dís.
Bhí biotáilte fairsing go leor, is beagán di a hól sa tír,
Is dá n-ólainnse galún Uí Dhónaill, b'fhurast mo scór a dhíol.

I was not long in the tavern until the young ones flocked to the
    house,
every one of them, a glass in their hand, to wish good luck to
    the couple.
Lashings of liquor there were there, none finer to be got in the
    land,
should I drink a gallon of O'Donnell's, my bill would be easy to
    pay.

In the manner of most of the native poets Peadar hints he's a rake – which, in truth, he wasn't:

> Agus muid istigh i dtigh an óil, d'fhiafraigh an óigbhean díom,
> 'Cá háit a mbíonn tú i dó chónaí, nó an gcoinníonn tú cró duit féin?'
> 'Ó, caithimse seal i dtigh an óil, is ní dhéanaim aon lón den phingin,
> ach am méid a shaothraím so ló, a chaitheamh le sport na hoíche.'

> And while we were still in the tavern the young girl made question of me,
> 'Where is it you usually live? Do you have a wee house of your own?'
> O, the pub is the place for me – I'm not one who pockets the pennies;
> what I earn in the course of the day I spend in the sport of the night.'

Going off not knowing where she might end up did not appeal to Nora, but the poet sought to drive worries on that score clean out of her head:

> Ag fanacht go ndéanaimis lón, caithear cuid mhór dár saol.
> Is fearr dúinn toiseacht go hóg, is beidh cuidiú dár gcóir arís.
> Má leanann tú mise sa ród, ní heagal duit buaireamh an tsaoil,
> beidh mise ag cruinniú an lóin, is geobhaidh tusa lóistín saor.

> Most of our life would be wasted, waiting until we'd gathered enough.
> Better to start out when we're young; help'll never be far from us.
> If you come on the road with me, you won't fear the stresses of life;
> I'll be amassing the money and the lodgings you'll get will be free.

But Nora wasn't going to be taken in that easily. She felt they'd
be better off staying in the island; they shouldn't stir out of it:

> Dá leanainnse thusa sa ród, ba ghairid go dtógfá díom.
> Bheifeása ag imirt is ag ól, is ba ghairid ár lón den phingin.
> Ach fan ar an bhaile 'mo chóir, is bí ar an nós linn féin,
> is geobhaidh tusa talamh go leor, is mise go deo mar mhnaoi.

> Striding before me on every highway, you soon would lose
> interest in me.
> Carousing and drinking night after night, our money would
> soon disappear.
> Set up house with me here in the island and live like one of our-
> selves,
> Acres of Arran's best arable land and me for your wife ever-
> more.

Even though they never married, Peadar praised Nora to the
skies when he said:

> Ní thig liom a moladh le feabhas, is í a mhearaigh 's a bhreoigh
> mo chroí,
> Níl aon duine dá bhfeicfeadh an tseoid, nach raigh chun bróin
> 'na díth,
> A leithéid ní fhacas go fóill, aon bhealach nó ród dá mbím,
> is dá bhfeicfí i mBéal an Átha Móir í, bheadh cailíní óga ar
> phingin.

> I can't find praises enough for her – she sears and bewilders my
> heart.
> Anyone who'd see this jewel would be distraught for the want
> of her.
> The likes of her I've never seen any place or road I've ever
> travelled on,
> If seen in Ballinamore, the local girls wouldn't rate as much as
> a penny.

'That was great praise for anybody, but my story's not finished yet. It's likely there were young girls on the island who were jealous of Nora because the poet lavished such praise on her, and they must have been far from pleased with him, but they couldn't have been half as annoyed as the girls in Ballinamore who found themselves dumped in 'the ha'penny place'. The Arranmore girls composed a verse of their own, lampooning Peadar for praising their neighbour Hughdáin's, daughter so highly:

> Ná bac le fear an chin mhóir, an rógaire réidh gan rath.
> Mura stada sé 'e mholadh iníon Hiúgó sa cheol,
> is ag cáineadh mhná óga an tsaoil,
> beidh sé mar *Neddy* go fóill, ag tarraingt an tslabhaic 's á dhíol.

> Pay no heed to that swell-headed, smooth-talking rascal.
> If he'll never cease praising that daughter of Hugo's
> and criticising every girl that he meets,
> he'll be no better than *Neddy* pulling sloak for to sell.

Anyway, he had to compose a special song to celebrate the girls of Ballinamore before they forgave him – if indeed they ever did forgive him! But it's likely they did; sure, didn't he end up marrying one of them!

THE NIGHT OF THE BIG WIND

It was Sunday, 6 January in 1839; it was the Feast of the Epiphany. The Búistéir was barely thirteen then, but again and again in his old age we heard him recount the horror and the devastation of that night. The tempest arose and raged on into the next day. Few people went to bed that night and those that did go to bed got little sleep between then and morning. The gale was west by north-westerly. It was difficult for sturdily built houses to withstand a storm like that, but whether your house was strong or not, no one had the nerve to venture out to secure anything. Even though the houses were low set in those days, they were in danger of being destroyed bringing the roof and beams down on the people huddling round the fire. Few people owned byres or barns then, and the cow, the calf and the donkey were tied down at the bottom of the house. The Búistéir often told us his father thought of taking a ball of straw ropes and fastening the roof with them, but his mother absolutely forbade him to go outside. Anyhow, he had no light of any sort and on a night like that it would be dangerous to carry out a light from the fire. The Búistéir and the other children went to bed, but their father and mother stayed up by the fire saying the rosary. Somehow or other they got through the night.

By morning great destruction had been done. Stacks were blown down, boats wrecked on the shore, or swept wherever the storm took them; the wells in the island were full of salt-spray, and so on. It was a terrifying night.

Even though the Búistéir slept little that Sunday night long ago, he was up early on Monday 7 January. Young and old alike rendered thanks to God for delivering them safe from the horrors of the night. Neighbours and relatives went to each other's house to find out how they'd got through the night. Even though they were exhausted, they couldn't stop talking about the night just past. The oldest of them could recall nothing like it. It was far, far worse than the Night of Seán McSorley, the Night of the Tor Buí, or any other night there had ever been.

Then, well on in the day, after dinner-time, they were astonished to see a small sailing ship out behind the Stag Rocks and it seemed she was trying to head for the shelter of Arran Roads. That was a mind-boggling sight then, and it still is mind-boggling today: that a vessel as small as that could survive the Night of the Big Wind was truly amazing. There were coastguards in Eighter and Arranmore at that time and they had no doubt about the shape they saw between them and the sky to the north. She was the *Andrew Nugent*, and her fame has lived on in people's minds ever since. She was built thirteen years earlier in Portaferry in County Down and was owned by a Sligo company; she was on her way to England when she was hit by the storm. Earlier in her career she plied between Ireland and Canada and the United States. She certainly wasn't a big vessel – just some hundred and sixty tons. She left Sligo on Sunday morning with a cargo of various sorts of food – cheese, butter, pork, eggs and so on and was probably out off Arranmore when the storm struck her. She endured a fierce night until morning. Her sails were torn away and she was taking water – you could say she was ripped apart by the fierce gale and the sea. A boat like her would have a crew of nine or ten, but God knows how many of them were still alive after that night. Only four or five were seen on deck when she came up to Calf Island.

It was almost impossible to navigate her on a day like that. The sailors and the captain by this stage were absolutely exhausted; the wind still raging, the sea was still up. It took her a long time to come up Arran Roads. It was close to four o'clock and night was falling before she made it as far as Calf Island. As soon as the Pollawaddy people saw her coming up, they made ready a small boat to pilot her into the anchorage, where she could be moored until morning. If they got a chance, they'd take her in to the harbour at Rutland Island; she'd be safe there no matter how ugly the weather would get. But conditions were so bad that afternoon they hadn't the slightest chance of making it as far as Rutland Island. In case the captain might not know the route, the coastguards lit two fires, one on Eighter and the other at Pollawaddy to direct them on their way up; that's how they managed to get as far as Calf Island.

It was there that the pilot, Tom O'Donnell, boarded her. The afternoon was rough and darkness was falling, and as soon as O'Donnell succeeded in getting aboard, the crew of the small boat that had brought him out went back ashore. Tom's job now was to bring the *Andrew Nugent* as far as the anchorage, moor her there, and stay on board until morning.

They headed for the anchorage, about half a mile away, but they didn't manage very well. They had to make their way through a narrow channel and with the wind and the sea as they were, it wasn't easy to get there before night. It's also said they struck a submerged reef known as the Blind Rock on their way up.

Very late in the afternoon they managed to reach the anchorage. Everything now appeared satisfactory. The boat was moored and she ought to be safe there until morning. Since the captain and the sailors who had survived thus far were exhausted, you'd say they would be able to go to bed and snatch a little sleep, and O'Donnell the pilot would keep an eye on everything overnight. But we don't know what they did, and that is something we'll never know. The ship was there when people went to bed and everyone was convinced that they had won the battle at last. But it didn't work out that way.

Sometime during the night the wind veered due north and the *Andrew Nugent* was now in a hopeless position. She must have dragged her anchor or the chain broke; the current and the gale brought her into the narrows, where she wouldn't be safe or sound much longer. It was pitch dark then and they weren't sure where they were. Even in daylight they wouldn't have been able to do anything. She struck Sionnach Point on the coast of Rutland Island and next morning all that was seen was her bow and her mast. The *Andrew Nugent* was lost and not even one person survived. Lost along with the crew was the pilot who had brought them as far as the anchorage – Tom O'Donnell.

The captain's name was Hugh Crangle. He was only fifty-three, and he's buried in the burial ground in Templecrone on the mainland. From all reports he had a large funeral and the parish priest, Father James McDevitt, conducted the graveyard ceremonies. No memorial stone marks his grave, but they tell me his name is inscribed on a tomb in his native place – Portaferry, County Down.

The same Father James McDevitt, An Sagart Rua, parish priest of Lower Templecrone, did not live long himself. In January 1847 at the height of the Great Famine he went to anoint a dying man, a tramp, or 'man of the roads', who was very ill and lying in a barn at Meenanalbany on the southern shore of Lough Meela near Burtonport. An Sagart Rua contracted the fever himself and died shortly afterwards. He was of the McDevitt family in Glenties and his remains were taken by horse and cart to Glenties where he is buried in the old graveyard.

There is a rock in Dungloe Bay. It is a high rock that remains uncovered even at high tide. The morning after the sinking of the *Andrew Nugent* there was a box of butter lying on the rock and it could only have come from the *Andrew Nugent*. The rock now had a new name – Carraig an Ime – The Butter Rock.

The Búistéir often told us when we were children that 8 January 1839 was an extraordinary day, the day the news got around that the *Andrew Nugent* was lost. There wasn't a creek or a cove but was full of her wreckage – butter, cheese, pork and so on. As well as that the old people used to tell us that the hulk of the ship could be seen like a black patch under the water near Sionnach Point – the place where she foundered during the night of the Big Wind long ago.

THE *FOREST MONARCH*

I'd often heard tell of the *Forest Monarch* when I was a child. The Búistéir mentioned it frequently, and my mother herself in her youth used to refer to the loss of that ship. If she let a bowl slip from her hands and it smashed on the floor, she'd gather up the pieces in her apron and say: 'A plague on it, I'd no time for it. Anyway, it's only an old bowl, and that's small loss compared to the *Forest Monarch* long ago on Iniskerragh.'

So it's no wonder I'm familiar with the story of this ship, for she was talked about round the fire at home, and anything I didn't learn there I picked up from the people of Iniskerragh when I was hired out there in my young days.

The Búistéir used to tell us the *Forest Monarch* ran aground on the west of Iniskerragh the year after the Famine. Judging by his account he was about twenty-three then, and he was one of the people brought across to Iniskerragh to salvage as much as they could of the ship and her cargo.

She was a large three-mast sailing ship, some 1,500 tons, this vessel that left her bones in Iniskerragh, long, long ago. With a cargo of timber she left New Brunswick in Canada outward bound for Scotland. She was wrecked in the month of November, and according to Iniskerragh folklore she was three weeks out from Canada at that stage.

Early in the morning, at about six o'clock she struck the

coast. The people in Iniskerragh used to say she first struck the Green Island off Arranmore, and was then carried by the wind and current as far as Iniskerragh. That morning was pitch black and the captain wasn't sure where the ship was taking him. There was no lighthouse on Arranmore at that time, and the captain hadn't a clue where he was. Luck was against him: though he managed to bring her as far as that, the west coast of Iniskerragh is a mass of reefs and all sorts of rocks; if she foundered among them, not a single member of the crew would escape with their life. She ploughed in through the narrows and got stuck there.

The islanders were asleep, but the commotion soon woke them up. They lit their lanterns and went across to the seashore. There was the *Forest Monarch* with all her lights ablaze and the sailors doing their best to get off. The crew numbered about thirty, and in spite of the angry seas, the darkness and every other sort of danger the sailors all made shore safely.

The captain wasn't the last man to leave the ship; no, the last sailor off was a black man. Making a huge effort he managed to save himself, and he claimed that neither the captain nor the crew made the least effort to rescue him. That's what he stated anyway. He pursued the captain all over the island with his knife drawn, and the captain had trouble keeping out of his reach. The houses on Iniskerragh were all strung out in a line, each one joined to the next. Every house had two doors, and the pursuit went in one door and out the other. At that time the houses were extremely low, so the doors were low too – maybe no more than five and a half feet. The big black man had to bend under every lintel and the pursuit of the captain continued like this until finally they came to a house where the doors were not only low but narrow as well. Making a

A group of Iniskerragh men leaving for Dungloe fair long ago. It was always held on the fourth day of the month, and the Iniskerragh men often left the evening before, especially if they had cattle for sale. There's a cow aboard as they prepare to set off.

great effort the black man managed to squeeze through the door, but he lost sight of the captain in the darkness. The captain hid from him and that's how he managed to escape the vengeance of the black sailor.

Later on in the day all the sailors went to bed for they were totally exhausted after all they had come through since the day before. It's true to say they went to bed, but one of them didn't sleep a wink – the wretched captain himself. As long as he was in danger from the black man, he couldn't sleep. As soon as he felt all the rest of the crew were asleep, he got up and put on his clothes. He explained why he was afraid, and offered the islanders five pounds to leave him out on the mainland so as not to be killed by the black man. The weather was still rough, but five pounds was five pounds, a very tempting sum in those times, and they dearly wanted to earn it if at all possible. They launched a boat and four or five of them landed him safely at Termon.

Foster of Roshine was controller of wrecks, flotsam, jetsam, etc. for the entire west of the county; it was his duty therefore to come to Iniskerragh and salvage the *Forest Monarch*, if any salvage was possible. He brought a gang of men from Arranmore and the mainland to help in his task. The coastguards from Arranmore and Inishcoo were there as well. It was obvious that there wasn't the slightest chance of getting the *Forest Monarch* afloat again, so they attempted to remove her cargo and salvage anything else of value. She was firmly wedged where she was lying, but with the force of the tides and the wind she was rocking and swaying back and forth and was in imminent danger of ripping apart and her cargo would be swept away to the east and west.

Her tall masts were no help; they were extremely heavy and the ship swayed this way and that whenever there was a strong gust, so they felt it was best to cut them down and lay them on the shore. That put an end to her rocking, so it was easy for them now to recover her cargo of timber. The timber was taken to Inishcoo Island and auctioned there. The priests bought a lot of it, and it's possible that that's the timber they roofed the churches in Kincasslagh and Dungloe with.

There was a fine glass cabin on the deck of the *Forest Monarch* and when it was dismantled, Foster took a fancy to it. This was the cabin where the captain and the ship's officers plotted courses and other matters. It was made of oak and

Roshine Lodge in Burtonport. It was the dwelling of Francis Foster (Foster of Roshine), the landlord's agent. Dr William Smyth lived in the lodge later.

had lots of glass panels on its sides, and seeing it Foster had an idea: 'If I were to take this cabin home, I'd turn it into a glass-house or a summer house.' And that's what he did: he took it across to Arranmore and set it up in front of his house in Leabgarrow. The next landlord in the island – Charley Beag – made use of it too, and it was still there later on when The Glen House was sold. But when Jack Boyle arrived there in 1922, he bought The Glen House to make an hotel of it; the cabin was dismantled, and he built the bar from its fine oak wood. That's why you'll find relics of the *Forest Monarch* in the Glen Hotel in Arranmore to this very day.

THE NIGHT OF THE MOLLIES

It was an afternoon in mid-May. I had just returned from the Lagan where I had been hired out for the winter. I had now obtained a place on Seán Taig's squad for the potato season and I'd have three weeks at home before I'd go to Scotland. I had just come in on the boat and we were sitting round the fire drinking a bowl of tea. I began to tell them – my mother, the Búistéir, Máire and Nancy – about my year away from home. The Búistéir was sitting there at the side of the fire, pipe in mouth, listening like someone who had never been away from home. I was telling them about the awful road between Lifford and Dungloe, with nothing but potholes and big rough stones on it. At that the Búistéir butted in and said something that set us all roaring with laughter. Said he: 'I'd bet those were the same stones we left behind us long ago in Lifford Jail. The only thing we did all the time we were there was breaking boulders in the town square. By the time we left there was a pile of stones there the height of Ailsa Craig off Girvan.'

My mother was smiling brightly. The Búistéir believed the prison authorities sold the stones to the grand juries of Counties Tyrone and Donegal, and that those are the stones you'll find on the roads today. Maybe so. But as regards the Búistéir, why, for better or worse, was he sentenced to jail? Well, it's quite a long story. The Búistéir himself would often refer to this adventure from long ago when there'd be storytelling at night round the fire.

As I mentioned already, during the Famine Conyngham the landlord sold his Arranmore estate to the new man, John Stoupe Charley. Charley was married to Mary Stewart Foster, Foster of Roshine's daughter, and when the couple came to the Rosses, they lived out in Roshine Lodge. Charley was constantly in and out of Arranmore, but he hadn't a residence there yet. So, two or three years after coming to Roshine Lodge he built the large house – The Glen House – for himself in the place Foster of Roshine had lived before then. As soon as the house was ready, Charley and his family moved in. Among the things he established were schools, a courthouse, a barracks for the police, a surgery, a post office and things like that. Like all landlords, he had an agent to administer the estate. Hugh Montgomery was his first agent; he was a married man and he lived on the island with his wife and family. According to the Búistéir the wife was called Margaret and they had four children. They were living in Fallagowan, the house Eamonn Sweeney lives in today. Montgomery's duties were to issue orders to the bailiffs, strike rents and collect them, adjudicate and settle any disputes over land.

The Arranmore people fared much worse under the new landlord than under Conyngham. Conyngham resided in a castle in Slane, County Meath, and his agent, Foster of Roshine, lived in Burtonport. But the new man 'Charley Beag' and his agent Hugh Montgomery were now living on the island in the midst of the tenants. In that way the new landlord could control them and spy on them; the agents and bailiffs before them – for better or worse – weren't able to

The post office as it was long ago. Before the hotel was opened visitors lodged there – among them Peadar O'Donnell, teacher on the island, 1916–18 and Thomas Ban Concannon, promoter (Timire) of Conradh na Gaeilge. Róise worked there frequently. Today it is a youth hostel.

do that. No wonder this new policy didn't please the tenants, and Hugh Montgomery the new agent wasn't in the least to their liking. Charley and his agent, however, had the law of England behind them, and there was little the tenants could do to remedy the situation. Landlords in those days could do what they pleased.

It was virtually impossible to make landlord Charley change his ways, for a Royal Irish Constabulary (or constabulary as they were known then) barracks was established in Pollawaddy to protect him from anyone who might interfere with him. Since that was the way matters stood, the only way the people could improve their lot was to ask the Molly Maguires for help; that's what the secret society was known as in those times. They were often called Gráinne's People as well – (after

Granuaile – Gráinne Ní Mháille). They were very strong throughout Donegal and were ready to help tenants who were being harshly treated by landlords, agents, bailiffs or the like. It seems likely there was a branch of the society on the island, for their brother members on the mainland promised to support them against Charley and his accomplices.

The Mollies decided that the best plan was to go to Hugh Montgomery's house, give him a beating, and make an effort to persuade him to change his way of running the estate. They had everything arranged. After nightfall the members from the mainland would go into the island, meet up with their comrades there, and then proceed to Hugh Montgomery's house. They picked a spring night for the job. They met their comrades as arranged, and some twenty of them headed up the slope in the direction of Hugh Montgomery's house. They reached the house sometime between midnight and one o'clock. They wore bright shirts and daubed their faces with soot to avoid detection. The people of the house were a bed when they arrived there and in the moonlight Hugh Montgomery was able to see them through the window when he woke up. Whoever was not there, the Búistéir clearly was there!

They smashed in the front door and a window at the back and in they went through the house. In former days the story was that they gave Hugh Montgomery a savage battering, but that wasn't the Búistéir's version. He used to tell us that they didn't as much as lay a finger on him. Definitely, the Búistéir knew every detail, for he was present that night, and afterwards he heard the evidence Hugh Montgomery and his wife presented in the courthouse in Lifford. Of the ten accused of breaking and entering eight came from Arranmore, the other two from the mainland. Charley and Hugh Montgomery swore they had never seen either of the two – Neil Campbell and John O'Donnell – previously. It's likely they crossed over to Arranmore with the Mollies that night.

In his evidence Hugh Montgomery stated that Paddy Coll – Paddy Mór from Illion, Paddy Mór na hUilleann – had a pistol, and that he fired a shot to frighten the people of the house. They stole one of his clocks and a safe containing twenty-four pounds. He further swore that Paddy Mór demanded ten pounds, and when Hugh Montgomery heard this, he asked his wife to give him five pounds to satisfy him. According to Hugh Montgomery's version Paddy Mór put the Bible in his hand, made him go down on his knees, and swear on the book.

They made him swear that from now on he'd erect no more fences so that the cattle and sheep of the island would be free to graze those areas the landlord had taken over for his own use. They also made him swear he never again would summons people whose cattle trespassed on the landlord's estate.

After that night the Pollawaddy RIC, Hugh Montgomery and Charley Beag, were busy. Some of the men were arrested here in the Rosses, more of them across in Scotland. Maurice Coll swore on the book that his son, Paddy Mór, never stirred from his house that night, but it's likely no attention was paid to his evidence. It was the court's verdict that all of them were guilty of the crime they were accused of; two of them were deemed worse than the rest – Paddy Mór of Illion and John O'Donnell from the mainland. Both of them were sentenced to four years' imprisonment and sent to Spike Island in Cork Harbour. Each of the other eight was sentenced to one year's imprisonment in Lifford Jail. And that's how it happened that the Búistéir spent a long hard year breaking stones in the square down there in Lifford all those years ago.

When Paddy Mór and John O'Donnell returned from Spike Island, people were amazed at how much English they had learned from the other prisoners. One day a woman who lived near O'Donnell remarked: 'John, John, didn't you pick up a quare deal of English and you away from home for only three years?' His reply set her laughing. 'Yes indeed, Máire, and from the way you put it, if I'd been away another year or two, I'd be back home a bishop or a priest.'

Hugh Montgomery never recovered from the fright he got that night. His wife and children were fearful all the time, and they had no intention of staying there any longer. They left the island very soon afterwards and Magee came in their place. Magee lived in that house after he came to the island and he had a post office there as well. As I said earlier, Charley introduced a daily postal service on the island, and his agent, Magee, was the new postmaster. He let half the house from then on to one of the Pollawaddy constables in case the Mollies might attack the house again. Much later in his life Magee left his house in Fallagowan and went to live in Leabgarrow. I'd say I was fifteen years old when Magee left the island for good.

What year was it then that the Mollies came to Arranmore? Well, we have a couple of pointers to tell us. The Búistéir – God grant he's happy – used to say he was about thirty-eight years old when he was in Lifford Jail. And a baby was born the night the Mollies came, and this person's age stamped the event right through his life. Charlie Boyle (Charlie Liam Hiúdaí) was the baby born that night. Many years later it was Charlie

Lifford's 'Black Jail' as it was long ago. The building that housed the prison was demolished in 1904, but the courthouse – the building on the right – still stands. The Búistéir and his companions stood trial there in 1863. Two of them – Paddy Mór Coll and John O'Donnell – were sentenced to four years' imprisonment. They were committed to Spike Island. Each of the others was sentenced to one year in prison; they served their sentence in Lifford Jail.

who became postmaster after Magee left the island. Charlie was born on 9 March 1863 – the night of the Mollies. That date fits in with the alibi the man from the mainland, John O'Donnell, gave in court, namely, that he was in Arranmore that night for he had recently distilled a quantity of poitín and that he went to Arranmore to sell some of it with a view to St Patrick's Day just a few days away. The same man was never short of a good excuse in any situation.

That was the time too when the schoolmaster on the island lost his job because he was linked with the Mollies and the fight against Hugh Montgomery and Charley. His name was Patrick O'Donnell; he was a native of Meenanalbany on the mainland. His mother's name was Cecily Mhacáin – she was one of the McCole Clan. This Patrick O'Donnell was related to my sister Máire's husband – Niall McCole from Acres.

Patrick O'Donnell was accused of writing a threatening letter against either Montgomery or Charley, and he was tried in Lifford. I believe this letter was found on Montgomery's doorstep after the night of the Mollies. Only one or two people on the island had any learning, so the RIC had no trouble investigating the case. The letter was attributed to the schoolmaster, but he strongly denied any part in it good or bad. In spite of that he was found guilty and sentenced to a year in jail on top of being sacked from his job. This happened in 1864. He served his sentence in Lifford and after his release he emigrated to Australia. His mother fell on hard times and died in the poor house in Glenties.

Now that Master O'Donnell was dismissed, there was a vacancy for a teacher on the island and that's when Daniel Boyle came here from Dungloe. He was in charge of the school when I was attending it. When he retired, Master Carr replaced him and I spent a couple of winters there as well when he was in charge of the school.

Charley and his family were scared out of their wits by the Mollies, and because of that the Pollawaddy policemen were very busy a long time afterwards. Night and day they were out on patrol in case anyone interfered with the landlord or his agent. A RIC man stayed a long time in the agent's house in Fallagowan, but I'm not sure if he was a lodger, or was quartered there or paid rent; there was usually a policeman close to the landlord's house in Leabgarrow as well.

There were eight policemen on the island then. They had their own boat to take them out and back from the mainland and they built a boathouse above the shore at Pollawaddy.

I heard the Búistéir say that these policemen used to go to Gweedore when there was trouble between the tenants and Lord George Hill the landlord. Every Monday six of them would go over to Gweedore and return to the barracks on Saturday. They'd cross to Burtonport on their boat, and they had to walk all the way to Gweedore and back, for the police were boycotted at that time and there wasn't a sidecar in the country that would carry them anywhere.

Most of the policemen stationed on Arranmore in those years came from the west of Ireland; they were chosen specially for the island and had to have at least some or a lot of Irish; furthermore, they had to be boatmen or have some knowledge of the sea.

THE CONGESTED DISTRICTS BOARD

Often in former times the old people could be heard talking about 'the time of the Congested' or 'the time of the Board' – the Congested Districts Board. This board was founded by the British government to help impoverished areas in the west of Ireland. It was set up when I was a young girl and it continued until our own government was set up in Dublin.

The board provided great help in its time. Remember, there was no dole, no children's allowance, no old age pension, no widow's pension, or any other kind of money to be got. To stay alive the people depended on fishing, earnings in Scotland, knitting and the crops. Our soil in the Rosses was poor and only through fierce struggling could we win any kind of crop from it. Much of it was burned land and without plenty of manure – seaweed, wrack and farmyard – it was hardly worth sowing at all. There was just one industry in the Rosses that was worth anything – the fishing industry – and the Congested Districts Board helped it enormously.

A year or two after I was born an attempt was made to revive this industry in the Rosses. Long before this there had been something similar, but it collapsed. Father Bernard Walker and William Hammond, Landlord Conyngham's agent, got the industry going again sometime around 1880.

*Having a smoke and a chat, Edward or Eamonn Sweeney
from Gortgar and Paddy Joe Gill from Brockagh in the district
of Dungloe. Patrick was a cattle dealer and he often came into
the island. Edward was married to Máire Ward, daughter of
Seán Taidhg and Máire, daughter of Master Boyle.*

Similar schemes were carried out in Burtonport, Gortnasade, Magheraroarty and other places around the coast. This was a great benefit to fishermen, for now they could land their catch, board their nets or unload them, pull their boats up and so on. The board built a quay at Aphort on the west side of Arranmore. A quay was a very handy place for landing seaweed or wrack; the kelp-gatherers were delighted of course.

Luggers were supplied to fishermen on the mainland and on Arranmore, and these large boats were far more useful than the small boats they fished from before. About a dozen of these boats came to our parish and four of them were given to fishermen in Arranmore. No wonder the fishing industry enjoyed a new boom under the Congested Districts Board.

Fishing instructors were brought from Scotland to Kincasslagh and other places to teach young fishermen their trade. They learned all about boats, about sailing, how to repair and mount nets, how to shoot and board them, and other skills like these. A barrel factory or cooperage was established out in Burtonport, and a big number of youngsters learned the cooper's craft. Buyers and fish-salters came to Burtonport, Kincasslagh and Rutland Island, and the Rosses people learned all about the herring trade – gutting, salting, packing in barrels, and so on.

While I was hired out on Iniskerragh, the great fishery in Traighenagh got under way. It lasted fifteen years but the herring left a year or two after I got married. All through those years the bay was teeming with fish, and there wasn't a boat in this area that didn't go up there every day while the shoals were in. The herring were brought up to Burtonport or Rutland Island where they were sold, but sometimes they were sold up on Marameelan quay.

Rosses fishermen selling salmon in Kincasslagh before the First World War.

A large company – the Donegal Fishing County – was operating in Rutland Island at that time; it was a great benefit to the Rosses fishermen. The men behind it were John L. Sayers and Samuel Guthrie; the people still speak highly of them. They bought every kind of fish there – herring, salmon, lobsters. I'd say the Donegal Fishing Co. received help from the Congested Districts Board, and it would be a shame if they didn't, for they were a huge help to the local fishermen. Another great boost for the fishery was the train – the Lough Swilly they called it – and it plied between Derry and Burtonport from 1903 on. And we mustn't ignore or forget there were ships leaving Burtonport for Glasgow every week with eggs, lobsters, fish and so on. Yes, our life was getting better bit by bit.

Under the board the fishermen had an entirely new life. In the years before I married, Arranmore fishermen used to go

*Herring workers in Kincasslagh, summer 1928. Salt herring were
exported to Germany, Poland and other European countries.*

west as far as the coast of County Mayo in search of herring.
And now men from the Rosses and Gweedore were travelling
to Connacht and County Clare to teach their fishermen the
craft, the same as the Scottish instructors had done here years
earlier.

The Congested Districts Board had its own ship – the
Granuaile – and it was often round the coast of Donegal in
those years. One summer day long ago I saw her moored in
Arran Roads when we were on our way out to the Westport
boat that would carry us to Scotland and the potato work. The
Granuaile carried materials and tools around the coast wherever
they were needed for the board's work. Bishop O'Donnell –
later Cardinal O'Donnell – was a member of the board at that
time and he helped the people of this county greatly. Had it
not been for the bishop, the board wouldn't have done as much
work for Donegal as it did – and that's a fact.

I've said it again and again, our roads in Donegal were a

disgrace before the board started its work. The roads were as rough as the seashore. Grants were given for the construction of new roads here and there. A new road was made between Dungloe and Crolly, another to Cloghwally and another to Keadue. An iron bridge was built across the Gweebarra river and another across to Cruit Island. Here in Arranmore the road to the lighthouse was extended, the road west to Aphort was added to and the same was done to roads in Pollawaddy and in Screig an tSeabhaic on the north side.

There was a pressing need for improvements in people's houses, and the board attempted to do that along the entire west coast of the country. I may say that at the end of the last century the people's houses hadn't changed much from what they were just after the Famine. With the help of the board the houses gradually improved. Not only were lots of new houses built, the ones that were there were smartened up. Up until then the people had thatched roofs, but the board helped them to roof them with felt in place of the straw or bent grass you saw everywhere up to that time.

Fever was widespread throughout the Rosses in those years, and it was often caused by bad water and by bad housing. In many places the cattle were still housed or tied down at the end of the dwelling houses with the result that there was a dung heap next to the gable. In many cases there was a pool of manure close to the door; that being the way things were, no wonder there still was fever everywhere. The parish priest, Monsignor James Walker, and Doctor Smyth went to extreme lengths to persuade them to build byres and barns on a new site, a reasonable distance from the dwelling-house, so that it would be much easier for them to keep the area next to the house clean. Board officers helped them in this matter too. Frequently there was no clean water in villages; that too spread diseases. The board sank wells here and there in the island to improve people's hygiene and health.

There was no nurse on Arranmore at that time. The board set about providing that type of service, for the population of the island was very large and there was no resident doctor. They built a house for a nurse and the first nurse arrived in 1901; we've had a nurse here ever since.

Purchasing the island for £8,500 from Mrs Charley, the landlord, was, I believe, the greatest thing the board did. The board and the land commission came to an agreement over the rent to be levied on the tenants from now on. The excessive rates of former years were scrapped, and annual rates of payment were agreed that weren't oppressive. Charley's people left the island and I must say their departure didn't distress us in the least. Magee, the landlord's agent, left as well, and the RIC and the coastguards weren't far behind him. We didn't miss them at all; we've managed our own affairs extremely well ever since.

When the board bought Charley's estate in Arranmore, great changes occurred in the possession of land. Up to the very end two-thirds of the hill pasture on the island remained in the possession of the landlord in spite of the threat from the Mollies long ago, and no one had permission to deprive him of it. There was a high fence around the hill, and none of his tenants had grazing rights inside that fence. If the landlord or the bailiff found a cow or a sheep grazing inside the fence, the animals were impounded and the owner couldn't repossess them until he paid a penalty of one shilling for each beast. Hardly any tenants had permission to cut turf there either. If someone was on his way to the lighthouse, he wasn't allowed to walk across the bog; he had to stay on the path where the main road runs today. That all came to an end now. The people were free to let their stock graze on the hill and they were free to cut turf there. They could now keep more sheep and cattle, and that meant they had much more milk and wool, and plenty of turf as well.

The board divided up the landlord's farm at Rannagh and in the Dreen (An Draighean) among people here and there in the island who were short of land. The board sent a surveyor called O'Malley to carry out this work; the old people still speak highly of him. As well as making alterations in the ownership of land, he erected a high fence along the top of the cliffs to stop sheep falling over.

The schemes carried out by the board in those years brought money to the islanders – to some a little, to others a lot. They employed men to work on the roads, to build the pier at Aphort, to build boundaries and erect fences, to sink wells, and so on. They were paid only twelve shillings and six pence per week then. I remember my sister's husband, Niall McCole, talking about the wages in that period. He worked on the construction of the railway line into Burtonport, and all they were paid was half a crown per day, fifteen shillings per week. If a man went labouring for anyone throughout the country at that time – say, digging potatoes, working at the turf, mowing, things like that – he'd receive only two shillings per day, and, believe me, a day meant a day – from darkness to darkness! God be praised, people have a better life today. The Congested Districts Board was a fine help to us in our day.

DR WILLIAM SMYTH

I was twenty-two years old when Dr Smyth died in 1901. I saw him hundreds of times on his visits to the island, and furthermore I went to him to have my hand lanced when I was hired in Iniskerragh. He also was the man who attended my father when we were living in Sheskinarone. He was very highly thought of when I was growing up and when he died there was widespread grief.

Dr Smyth was born in 1859 in Mountcharles, six miles from Donegal town. His father had a practice there. Having attended the Royal School in Raphoe, he went to Trinity College, Dublin, where he studied medicine. He died twenty years after qualifying as a doctor. Having obtained his degree in medicine he returned to practice in his native county – Donegal. In 1881 he was appointed dispensary doctor for the Ardara district, but after only one year there he came to practice in Burtonport. The elderly Dr Spencer had died from fever after six years in the practice and Dr Smyth was appointed in his place. Dr Spencer had lived in Roshine Lodge, the house the landlord's agent, Foster of Roshine, once owned, and after he married, Dr Smyth moved into that house too. During his student days in Trinity College, Smyth often visited the Rosses, for at that time he knew William Hammond who lived in Lackbeg House and was the landlord's agent. During these frequent visits to the Hammond family, he met Esther Keon, the daughter of William Keon, who had a shop and the post office in Burtonport. William Keon's brother Daniel had a store and the post office in Bunbeg. It is said that these people were invited to the county by the landlords during the Famine years and took over management of the shops under their protection. In any event, Dr Smyth married Esther Keon. They had thirteen children, five of whom died when young.

Dr Smyth had a huge area to cover in those days. Sometimes there wouldn't be a doctor in Dungloe, and that meant he'd often have to attend all the people of the Rosses, from Gweedore to Gweebarra. Furthermore, Arranmore had a large population, and there were people living on all the islands off that coast – on Inish Saille, Inishfree, Iniskerragh, Rutland, Eighter, Owey and still other islands. As well as that, there were no motor cars then and scarcely any motor boats. Summer and winter the only way he could get round the entire Rosses was by horse and trap. As there was no doctor on Arranmore, he had to call there regularly – once a week. Roads were extremely bad then and we ourselves could imagine the hardship involved in a journey from Burtonport to Traighenagh or Rannafast.

Dr Smyth was a powerful, athletic man, but his sturdiness and agility were all needed for the work he performed over twenty years. He was a big man – over six feet tall – and was keen on boating, swimming, hunting, games and everything like that. But he was particularly fond of boats, and used to organise boat-racing days in Burtonport and even in Arranmore itself. He had his own small sailing boat and did most of the rigging and steering. His sailing boat won the sailing race at the Arranmore regatta in 1900. Stella was his daughter and

Dr William Smyth (1859–1901).

the boat was named for her. He didn't find it easy to travel into Arranmore then, especially during the winter. As well as that, he had to moor his boat in deep water while on duty in the island and when his day's work was over he'd have to go back out to the boat again. The winter day was extremely short and he found it difficult to get much work done at that time of year. Since 1923, we have a resident doctor on the island, and now, thank God, we have a hospital in Dungloe, and that's a great help to young and old.

But in 1901 the cruellest misfortune occurred in Dr Smyth's

life. That autumn there was an outbreak of fever in Arranmore. The family of Joe Gallagher or Joe Antain in Ballintra were struck by the dreadful disease, typhus, or the black fever (*an galar dubh*) as the people called it. Joe, his wife and their five children were living there beside the river. The fever attacked them and there was little hope for them. That was the year the first nurse was appointed to the island – Nurse Connolly – but apart from her, Dr Smyth had no assistance. It was the end of autumn too, and it was already obvious that the days were shortening and winter was on its way. Night and day Joe Antain's family were a worry to the doctor. He was calling on them as often as he could, but they were in such a plight that he found it impossible to provide the care they needed. He decided therefore it was best to bring them out of the island altogether and send them to Glenties hospital.

He managed to obtain an old boat and prepared to cross into Arranmore, take the Gallaghers out and send them to the hospital. It was the only boat he could get for this job, for the boatmen round about weren't willing to offer their boats in case they or their families would catch the fever. He received help from Brendan McCarthy the county doctor, Harry Hammond of Burtonport and Séimí Boyle the relieving officer in Dungloe. As I say, it was an old boat for this job, and even though she took lots of water on the way in and out, they kept on bailing so there was no danger of her sinking. The big fishery at Traighenagh was busy at the time, and when they arrived at Burtonport, there was a huge number of boats along the quay. It was only a small quay then – the railway quay wasn't built yet. The fishermen kept well away from them, so great was their fear of the disease. They managed somehow to get the Gallaghers out of the boat, and they were sent to Glenties in

Dr William Smyth, his wife and family. Mrs Smyth died in Bangor, County Down in 1962.

an ambulance. The Gallaghers all recovered afterwards, thank God.

A week or so later the doctor felt some sort of sickness working on him. He reckoned he was worn out by too much work and decided to go off on holiday for a week or two. Four vessels plied between Burtonport and Glasgow at that time – the *Tyrconnell*, the *Carricklee*, the *Ballyness* and the *Burtonport*; I think it was the *Burtonport* he travelled on. But having arrived in Glasgow his health grew much worse. Instead of entering a hospital in Scotland, he decided to come home. He had spent only two days across there.

He took the boat to Derry and after that travelled up on the train to Fintown. As he was leaving Derry that morning, he sent his wife a wire to have the horse and trap meet him that night at Fintown railway station. It was done as he requested.

It was a cold, rough evening in the middle of November and to top all the woes of the evening the rain started lashing as they were leaving the station. It was midnight when they arrived at Roshine Lodge. The doctor was frozen and totally exhausted. He went to bed after his arrival, but was never to get up out of that bed again. Dr Gardiner had recently taken over in Dungloe and he was asked to call. He had no doubt about his fellow doctor's illness – it was typhoid, 'the black fever'. It's likely he picked up the disease while attending the Gallaghers in Arranmore. He was beyond recovery. He died on 19 November 1901, and was buried in the Protestant cemetery in Dungloe. His wife stayed on in Burtonport until 1934; then she left to live with one of her daughters in Bangor, County Down.

Dr Smyth gained the respect and honour of the people throughout his life; his name is treated with respect and admiration to this very day, for he was a man who put his own life in danger in order to help others. The Gallaghers survived, but Dr William Smyth – the man who saved them – died.

THE LOUGH SWILLY RAILWAY

The extension of the Lough Swilly Railway from Letterkenny to Burtonport was a great benefit to the people of the Gaeltacht. For twenty years before this the railway line from Derry came as far as Letterkenny, but the first train didn't come into Burtonport until March 1903. It was no wonder that young and old alike were overjoyed that day. That some such day would come had been talked about for ages, but it was difficult to realise that the railway would come as far as the Rosses in our own lifetime. Andy McGinley and the old folk of the locality used to recount the prophecies of Colmcille, and especially that section that said that 'a day would come when the black pig would run west to the sea'. That was confirmed at last. The train came in between the hills and glens of Donegal, as far as Burtonport on the west coast. The old people praised God for sparing them long enough to see such a wonder in their day. Life was totally changed, they thought.

The coming of the railway helped the people on the west coast in many different ways. Twenty years earlier, the train came no further than Stranorlar and the Rosses shopkeepers had to send carts as far as Ballybofey to bring back goods for shops in Dungloe, Burtonport, Annagary and other places like that. The carters had a long, wretched road to Ballybofey and they had to come back up that same road later in the day – often after nightfall. Sometimes on the way down, they carried goods like eggs and fish, but there were other times they carried nothing – they had just an empty cart. It's true that for fifteen years before the coming of the train ships sailed from Burtonport to Derry and Glasgow, but those ships depended on the weather and didn't come regularly in winter. These ships would bring flour, Indian meal, oatmeal and merchandise into Burtonport and would take out eggs and fish – the same as the men with the carts on the road to Ballybofey. When the railway came, there was no need for the carters any longer, but the ships kept the service going until the first Great War broke out.

Those who were travelling to Scotland, Letterkenny, Derry, Doon Well, or any destination at all in the two countries were really glad of the train. We appreciated it too, for we could travel to the Lagan on it, or across to Scotland, and come home the same way. It was much more convenient for the people of the island in summertime, for the weather would be fine then and the evenings long enough for us to reach home after getting off the train at Burtonport. But it would be a different story in winter: we'd have to spend the night there in lodgings, and if you were to leave for Scotland or the Lagan on the morning train, you had to come out of the island the night before and stay overnight in Burtonport in order to be in time. The boat for Scotland still came into Arran Roads every summer, but not as many would sail on her, for now you could take the train to Derry any day the notion took you, and go on to Glasgow that night on the Derry boat.

It's a fact worth mentioning that at that time young children who had never been away from home before used to go across to Scotland to the potato work; some of them were so young that they hadn't ever been in Dungloe or even Burtonport! And it's also true that Arranmore children long ago returning on the train up from Derry had never set foot in Burtonport till then! In the summer, those children would have gone on the Scottish boat from Arran Roads to work at the potatoes in Ayrshire, and would never have been outside the island before.

In our conversations round the fire by night it was remarked that many people departed by that very train and never came back again. Hundreds left for Scotland and America never to return. Unfortunately, the occasional one was killed; more of them married abroad and settled down; some others just went to the dogs and were never heard of again. Some were very successful; there were others, however, who found life just too tough. That old train certainly carried an astonishing number of passengers from 1903 right up to 1940, when the service was closed down in the second year of the Second World War.

One spring day in 1923 a group of twenty-five young men and girls left the island for America. They went to Chicago and no more than a quarter of them ever came back. Times were bad in Ireland then and times were bad in Scotland too, so they reckoned a better life was in store for them in America. But appearances can deceive. They weren't long in America, when things there took a turn for the worse as well; they were left destitute, didn't get a day's work, hadn't even a bite to eat. We all heard accounts of the depression in America from those who came home or from the letters that people wrote home.

People always held dances or get-togethers on the night before they'd leave for America. The young folk used to gather at their house to bid them farewell. Then late in the evening the old people would drop in to see them. The person leaving would do the rounds of the houses on the final two days to bid farewell to his friends and acquaintances. Often he'd receive a little present from his neighbours before leaving. And sometimes he'd be given presents for people from that area who had already emigrated: a pair of stockings, a jersey, gloves, things like that. As well as the dancing on the night before leaving, there was singing too. I was present at scores of these gatherings, and I often sang there as well. The songs that were sung on these occasions were usually sorrowful ones, so much so that if the person who was to leave in the morning wasn't downhearted, he or she certainly would be after listening to them through the night. One of these songs – *Noreen Bawn* – tells of a young girl from Donegal who went to America and returned home later, her health broken:

> There's a glen in old Tyrconnell, there's a cottage in the glen
> where once lived as fair a female as e'er inspired a poet's pen.
> But a letter came one evening with her passage paid to go
> to the land where the Missouri and Mississippi flow ...

Before the end of this song half the people of the house would be in tears and no wonder. And there was another song about a person who went to Australia:

> Far away in Australia I will be ever true,
> toiling each day in that land far away,
> building a home for you ...

And then, when they were leaving the house, they'd weep floods of tears, and they'd do the same again when leaving the quay for Burtonport. And it was the same again at the railway station in Burtonport: they cried in torrents. The Búistéir used to say to us that Burtonport Station should have been called 'The Platform of Tears', for more tears were shed there than in any graveyard in Ireland!

And now that I'm talking about the Lough Swilly train, I must say a word or two about the accident that befell that train near Creeslough in 1925. Four people were killed that night and many others were injured. The four who died were Niall Duggan from the parish of Termon, a lady from Falcarragh – her name was Una Mulligan, and two from Arranmore – Phil Boyle from Leabgarrow and his wife Sarah. It was the night before the eve of St Bridget's Day, namely 30 January 1925, and a gale was blowing that night as bad as any gale I ever experienced in my life; the wind was extremely powerful – a north or north-westerly. At about six in the evening the train left Letterkenny for Burtonport, but the accident happened about an hour and a half later as she was approaching Creeslough. She had to cross the large viaduct, the Owencarrow viaduct, there and that's where it happened. The wind was coming up the glen in powerful gusts and one of the carriages was blown off the rails and fell down ten feet from the high bridge. It fell amid rocks so most of it was shattered into smithereens; the four who died were in this carriage. It happened between seven and eight at night and since the night was exceedingly dark and the gale was fierce, it wasn't easy for the rescuers to reach the dead or wounded. But everybody did as much as they could.

Phil Boyle and his wife were on their way back from Dublin. At that time they owned a shop on the island and had gone up to Dublin on business. Returning from Dublin they visited the hospital in Letterkenny where their son – also called Phil – had been a patient since Christmas. He had had an accident while working in the Arranmore lighthouse and lost two fingers on one hand. He had now recovered and was coming home. He was in the carriage along with his father and mother, but thank God, he managed to survive. The father died instantly, but the mother lived another six hours before dying in Letterkenny hospital. It was her brother, Eamonn Gallagher, and six members of his family who were lost in the Arranmore Disaster ten years later in 1935.

The people of the island were grief-stricken when word came of Phil and Sarah's death; I personally was very sad, for I had been really close to them throughout my life and they truly were a pleasant and helpful couple in their time. Phil was a fine fiddler – he was the man who played for us on the night of our wedding party.

The island wasn't linked by telephone cable till 1938 – three years after the drowning in Béal an Éilín: there was absolutely no way of sending a telegram to Arranmore in 1925. On account of that it wasn't easy to send word about the deaths on the day after the accident at Creeslough. It was a rough day, what with wind and high seas, but a boat from Burtonport made a special trip to bring the news. When we saw the boat coming, it was clear that something serious made them put to sea on a day like that. Pat Dhonncha and his brother Dan brought us the dreadful news; they lived in Acres and were always friendly and obliging to the people of Arranmore. Dan looked after the boat down at the quay while Pat went up to Johnny Ban's house with the news. Johnny was a cousin of Phil's, and he was the one who had to break the bad news to the family and relatives of the dead couple. That night was the eve of St Bridget's Day and it's a night I'll never forget as long as I live.

THE WHALING STATION

Round about the time I got married trouble erupted over the whaling station in Arranmore. A company from Norway intended killing whales off the north-west coast of Ireland – our word for these creatures is *péistí* – and they chose our island as their base of operations. It's likely they never imagined any opposition to their scheme. Members of the company arrived here and got down to work. They purchased a plot of land from Jack O'Hara of Pollawaddy and made arrangements to build the station. There would be moorings there for their fishing boats beside Calf Island and moorings in the harbour at Rutland Island as well. They planned to construct a factory there, and wooden sheds, dwelling houses, a quay and so on. They appointed a local man – Niall Gallagher, the son of Eoghan Mhór – as their representative, and set about the project.

Men arrived from Norway and they commenced working. The Pollawaddy police barracks was vacant then, for the RIC had left thirteen years earlier, and the Norwegians rented the building and stayed there during their time on the island. More of them took lodgings in other houses and the rest of the Norwegians lived on their ships or boats moored in the harbour. No wonder the Pollawaddy people welcomed these strangers for they reckoned they'd be a Godsend to the district in many ways. There'd be work for the locals while the base was being built and work later on when the station was in production.

And, indeed, earnings of any kind were sorely needed at that time. The Congested Districts Board had done nothing for the Pollawaddy people. Yes, the board had built a new pier back in Aphort more than ten years before this, but they didn't spend a penny on the east side of the island. Pollawaddy wasn't to have a quay of any sort for another thirty years, and the lack of a quay hurt them fiercely. They had nowhere to berth their boats after coming ashore from the fishing. They had to haul their small boats up the shore when the day's work ended and they had to haul them down in the same way next morning. That was cruel, punishing work. So when these foreigners arrived, the local fishermen were delighted, for they were sure a new quay would be built that would in time be a benefit to them all.

Truth to tell, the Congested Districts Board had indeed thought of establishing a fishing port or station in Pollawaddy before this, but didn't go ahead with it. There were officers on the board who intended helping the people of the island and they felt there was no better way to do this than to aid the fishing industry on the island itself. To this very day all the fish has to be taken to Burtonport and sold there. Before the railway came to Burtonport the directors of the board were of the opinion that establishing a fishery port in Pollawaddy would be worthwhile; it would be possible to make supplies for the industry available there – barrels, salt, boxes and so on – and the fish could be sent off by sea to the market. The officers of the board believed that the Arranmore fishermen were spending too much of their money in the pubs in

Burtonport and Rutland Island, and the situation wouldn't be as bad if they had a port in Pollawaddy. But, even though the board thought along those lines long ago, nothing ever came of it. And once the train reached Burtonport, it was forgotten about completely.

The scheme to set up the whaling station here in Pollawaddy didn't quite please everybody. For some reason or other, the priests were not happy that Norwegians would be arriving there although Father Bernard Walker said at the inquiry that was set up that he initially supported the project. Others too, who had no connection with the sea or with the fishing industry, began to sneer at the project. Some people said that this type of operation would ruin the local herring fishery, for, they said, this had happened everywhere else in the world where such a station had been built. It's difficult to say truly what these people had in mind. Some, I believe, held sincere opinions, but many more were only looking after their own interest. In the main, this matter of the whaling station was a source of great disagreement at that time. Even on the island itself, people had different opinions on it. Those who lived beside the station were in favour of it, but those at a greater distance from it were either indifferent or objected to it strongly.

The Norwegians commenced work on the station, but no sooner had they constructed the temporary quay – a wooden jetty – than the work had to stop. It was announced that there was to be an inquiry to settle this contentious matter and that the work was to cease until the inquiry's verdict was made public. An inquiry committee was set up and evidence was taken from both sides. This committee sat for a week at Burtonport, and later at Derry, to gather all the evidence. After that, the government decreed that it was illegal to proceed with the station as planned by the company from Norway. That was the end of the story. The Norwegians had to quit the place without more ado. But even though the Norwegians left, the whole affair wasn't quickly forgotten, and it continued to be a source of argument for a very long time. Ever since then, the people of Pollawaddy saw the affair in this way: opposition was mounted to stop a project that would have benefited the area if it had been allowed to go ahead.

But the men from Norway weren't beaten yet. Leaving Donegal, they headed west for County Mayo and they fared much better there. They set up two stations – one in Inish Gé, the other in Elly Bay. Those whaling stations were very successful; nobody ever opposed them and the work went on there with their company, The Arranmore Whaling Company, up to 1923.

Even though this Norwegian company was in Arranmore just for one summer, they provided work for the locals during that time. The pay was low – half a crown per day – but there were people in the neighbourhood of Pollawaddy who had earned as much as eight pounds by the time the season ended. Because of that I'd say it wasn't right to oppose the scheme and bring it to a stop. I haven't the slightest notion if the normal fishing in County Mayo declined in any way because a whaling station was established on that coast.

THE YEAR OF THE YELLOW GRAIN

It was a couple of days before St Brigid's Day 1926 – the year the Búistéir died. I had completed the housework and Séimí and me were sitting and chatting at the fireside. Just then two children came to the door telling us a large ship was coming up the bay. That wasn't big news at that time, for ships often arrived at Burtonport with cargoes of flour from Cardiff or Liverpool. I stood up to look out the door. The instant I was unlatching the door, the ship's whistle sounded a distress signal as if she required pilots to the port or some other sort of help. I could see her as soon as I stood at the door. She was a large vessel, much larger than any ship I'd ever seen come up that channel, and she was all lit up. She was still under way, as if she were heading for the anchorage in Calf Island. When my husband came to the door and saw the route she was taking, he reckoned it wasn't deep enough and felt she'd strike a rock in her path very soon. He was right – inside a minute we heard the ship grinding and tearing against the rocks. 'By God,' said Séimí, 'she's after striking the Blind Rock.'

But she kept going until she got as far as the anchorage. There she stopped, and we heard the noise and jangling of the chains as if she were dropping anchor.

There wasn't a door around us but was open, the people all standing at the door and looking out at the ship. The

youngsters went off running down as far as the shore to see
what was going on. It was dark by this time and it wasn't fully
clear to us how things were, but we did know that small boats
were being launched to get out to her. Johnny Ban Byrne
from Leabgarrow and Charles O'Donnell, Charlie Tony from
Eighter Island, went aboard her. They started talking to the
captain, but they didn't understand each other very well. The
crew were Greeks and none of them had much English. It was
difficult to help them or offer them correct advice. One thing
they all understood: the ship was holed down under and was
taking water very quickly. If she remained where she was any
longer, she would go under very quickly. In the darkness of the
night the Greeks had no idea what kind of place they were at.
They wanted to run the ship ashore. They hurriedly left in the
direction of the White Strand. It seems likely they were able to
indicate their plan for saving the ship to the men who came out
to them. But when they got her under way, the steering failed
and she went completely out of control. Instead of beaching at
the White Strand, she charged in the direction of Leabgarrow
Beach. They failed to get her as far as the shore – she struck the
rear of the Great Creek Rock, and her skeleton has lain there
ever since. She was stuck fast and firm on those rocks, so tight
there was no way she'd ever get going again. The captain and
crew were safe. Because she had come from Greece, she was
never called anything but the Greek Ship.

People from all over the island, I can tell you, were in
crowds down there at the shore that night. The ship's engines
were now silent, but her lights were still blazing. The captain
wouldn't know how badly she was holed until she could be
examined in daylight. But rumours were already circulating
that there was two foot of water in her holds. Johnny Ban and

Leabgarrow in 1926. The Greek ship, the Elfinoris, *lies behind the rocks. In the centre, on the roadside, the post office.*

the others who had been aboard her knew she'd never budge from where she was any more. As one of them said when he came ashore: 'She's after making a bed for herself tonight, and that same bed will be her bed for ever.' He was right.

This ship was the *Elfinoris* and she was on her way from Braila at the mouth of the Danube with a cargo of maize. She was large – 5,000 ton. She had already discharged some of the maize at Belfast and was on her way to Sligo with the rest of the cargo when this happened. She began taking water between Tory Island and Arranmore and the captain believed it was best to make for some place on shore, where she could be repaired. That's what brought him into Arran Roads.

Bad as it was for her on the way in, she was infinitely worse off after striking the Blind Rock. She now began to ship water crazily and had to be given a run for the shore to ensure her safety. That plan failed when the steering packed in. After that it was all up with her.

The captain and his crew remained in Arranmore until it was obvious the *Elfinoris* could never be set afloat; they left for home. During their time on the island the only person who could hold a conversation with them was Dr Bartley Duggan, the priest of the island; nobody else could talk to them, nobody else had any Greek. He had been a padre in the British army in the First World War and he may have learned Greek then.

And what happened to her cargo of yellow maize? Paddy the Cope, Patrick Gallagher the manager Templecrone Co-Operative Store, bought the cargo from the insurers and took as much of it as was sound to his mill in Dungloe and had it ground into Indian meal. And the portion of the cargo that was only slightly damaged by the salt water was salvaged, dried and milled by him as well. He paid boatmen from the islands and the mainland to transport the yellow grain to the mill, and he sold most of it to boatmen from every part of the Rosses and Gweedore; they brought it home and sold it to any neighbours who had fowl and cattle. The grain was selling at a shilling a bag on the mainland. In Arranmore too a huge quantity of the grain was bought and they found it great feeding for hens and cattle. Milk and eggs were plentiful as long as the yellow grain lasted. We bought more than a ton of it. I used to lay it out in the sun to dry and I'd take it indoors before nightfall. But it has to be said the grain brought lots of rats and mice around as well.

It's an ill wind that blows no good to anybody. And so it was with us in the Year of the Yellow Grain. That grain was a great help to us. God be good to the Búistéir, he used tell us that away back in the past shipwrecks were longed for, that a ship in imminent danger was closely watched, and the only thing you'd hear people saying was: 'Trócaire Dé ar uair bhur mbáis – ach uair de spás nár fhaighe sibh (God be merciful to you in the hour of your death – but may you not be granted one hour extra)', as the cynic – you'll find one in every community – would tag on to the petition. But I'm sure no one made remarks like that on the night we're dealing with – 28 January 1926, the night of the *Elfinoris*.

Among the teachers on Arranmore at the time was a young man from the mainland – Patrick O'Donnell from Belcruit; he wrote a poem about the loss of the ship:

Ina luí go suaimhneach i ndiaidh a cuid siúlta,
gan cor ná lúb aisti faoi fholcadh na dtonn,
dálta na gcarraigeacha thart ar gach taobh di
atá ag sáthadh a gcár géar isteach fríd a bun.

Lying so peacefully after her journeyings,
No twisting, no stirring 'neath the sifting of waves,
Wedlocked to rocks that surround her on all sides,
That gorge their sharp teeth ever deep in her hull.

Chonaic sí an lá úd ar shnámh sí go héadrom
ar éadan na mara mar an fhaoileog ar toinn;
ach, mo bhrón, tá sí anois caite ar thráigh na Leibhe Gairbhe,
indiaidh theacht ón Domhan Thoir na mílte anonn.

There were days she had seen herself floating so lightly
On the brow of the sea as the gull skims the wave
But, alas, she's now foundered on the shore of Leabgarrow
Since leaving the East World all those miles far away.

B'iomaí troid léanmhar a chuir tú do chlaíomh ann,
is na tonntaí ag éire mar chruacha ar do shlí;
char shíl tú an uair sin go mbeifeá chomh híseal,
is na barróga go síor dod adhlacadh síos.

Many harrowing fights you oft thrust your sword in,
Billows rearing like mountain peaks barring your way;
Little you felt in those days you'd be left low
Crisp wave-tops eternally buoying your grave.

Ach sé deireadh gach aon rud a bheith 'na luí os íseal,
an long thíos faoin uisce is a corp ins an uaigh;
agus de thairbhe an bháid sin, má tá sí anois cloíte,
chonaic sí an lá a raibh aice an bhuaidh.

But it's marked out for everything finally to lie low,
The ship on the sea-bed, the corpse in the grave.
Be it said of that vessel, though now she is shattered,
There was a day once when victory was hers.

THE ARRANMORE DROWNINGS

Anyone who is interested in the question of migration, or those who have actually gone across year after year in search of work in Scotland will surely have heard tell of the terrible disasters migrants suffered down the years. Among those disasters is the drowning in 1894 of thirty-four migrants at Westport in County Mayo, just as they were about to leave for Scotland. The boat for Scotland was anchored some distance out from the harbour and the passengers had to be ferried to the steamer on a hooker. The hooker probably capsized and they were all flung into the water. Most of them were from Achill, bound for tattie-hoking in Scotland. The Mayo people told that tragic story over and over again as we sat chatting around the fire in the bothies; many of them were neighbours of those who drowned, some in fact were related to them.

Then, in the middle of September 1947, ten Achill people died in Kirkintilloch near Glasgow when their bothy caught fire. It's likely they were drying wet clothes around the fire that night; the clothes caught fire and the whole place went up in flames. There was a lock or heavy bolt on the outside of the door so there was no way they could open the door and flee from the fire. One of them was a boy who was only thirteen years of age. We had great sympathy for the poor creatures who perished, for all of us in our time had worked at the potatoes and we well knew the hardship they and their likes had to put up with across in Scotland.

However it was 9 November 1935 when the Arran drownings, or, as the newspapers headlined it, 'The Arranmore Disaster', happened. It was the custom then, exactly as it had been in our time and still continues today, for people to go across to Scotland at the beginning of June, and they'd be gone from home working at the potatoes through the summer and autumn. After that the squads would return in November. They always wrote home beforehand to let their relatives know the day to expect them. Round about two o'clock that afternoon, Saturday, a boat left Aphort on its way out to Burtonport to meet the people who had sent them word to be there that day. On Friday night these people had travelled on the Derry boat from Glasgow and on Saturday they were to take the train to Burtonport.

The boat that went out for them was small; she was only twenty-four feet long; there was no engine – just a sail and the four oars they'd need if they had to row out or back, something they had to do many a time down the years. I'd say the boat reached Burtonport quay some time after three, so they had a couple of hours to wait before the train arrived in the station.

Sailing boats seldom went to sea light-handed, least of all in winter, and these were the seven on board when she left Aphort pier that afternoon: Eamonn Gallagher, sixty-one – the man who owned the boat, his son Patrick, twenty-six, and another son Michael, twenty-nine; Seán Gallagher, twenty, son of Michael Gallagher; John Rodgers, thirty-four; Eamonn Ward, fifty-one, and John O'Donnell, fifty.

People bound for Arranmore usually travelled up to Burtonport on the early train so as to get home that night.

The Great Drowning 1935. Islanders on the day of the funeral.

Nobody likes taking risks at sea after nightfall, least of all in wintry weather. This train that pulled into Burtonport round about five had left Derry at eleven; she should have reached her destination at half-past three, but that train rarely arrived on time. Generally, she'd be more than an hour late, with the result that she wouldn't pull into Burtonport until sometime between half-past four and five o'clock. She carried freight as well as passengers, so there were delays at every station to off-load goods, and there were longer delays at certain stations where wagons had to be shunted. This particular afternoon she didn't arrive until ten to five, and the passengers then had to carry their baggage down to the quay two hundred yards away.

I reckon they wouldn't have been able to set off any earlier than a quarter past five. A five-mile journey lay ahead of them and they should have made Aphort pier by about a quarter past six. There were thirteen Arranmore people on the train that afternoon, and I'm sure they were greatly relieved to see a boat from the island waiting at the quay for them when they got off the train. A boat from Burtonport had been across in Arranmore that afternoon, but that boat was returning to the

The Arranmore Disaster. The bodies being borne up from Aphort Pier. The curate, Fr Barney Gallagher, and schoolmaster, Barney Gallagher alongside the first coffin.

quay just when the boat with the potato workers was ready to sail; that's why all the Arranmore passengers embarked on the same boat.

There were twenty in all on the boat, the crew of seven and the thirteen from the train; there were boxes and packages on the boat as well. It was a chilly evening when they moved away from the quay, and darkness was now falling. It was a winter's night, but the sea wasn't rough enough to worry them. A couple of small boats from Arranmore had been out fishing for pollock or coalfish in Arran Roads earlier that afternoon – something they'd hardly do if the sea was up or rough in any way. There was a favourable wind behind the boat on its way into Arranmore, but there were heavy wintry showers that evening, showers that would blacken the sky all around them if they were taken unawares. It's thought one of these showers

The funeral procession making its way to the graveyard. At the head of the procession are Canon McAteer, parish priest, and Fr Barney Gallagher, curate on the island.

struck them at Béal an Éilín half an hour later – the time the accident happened. We're not sure. At all events, some mistake was made at that point; there's nobody today who knows what led to that blunder.

In all nineteen people drowned – six of the crew who came out earlier that afternoon and the thirteen on their way home from Scotland.

These are the thirteen who arrived on the train that night: Maeve Gallagher, 28, Eamonn Gallagher, 24, Seán Gallagher, 22, Charlie Gallagher, 20, and Nora Gallagher, 16. These five were all members of the family of Eamonn Gallagher, the man who owned the boat.

Manus Gallagher, 17, Nora Gallagher, 21, and Daniel Gallagher, 27. These three victims were children of Michael Gallagher; their 20-year-old brother Seán was one of the crew who had come out from Arranmore that day.

250 - Róise Rua

13 November 1935 – the day of the funerals in Arranmore.
In the photograph are Canon McAteer, parish priest, Fr Dan Sweeney,
Fr Barney Gallagher, Fr Thomas Doherty and
the garda superintendent, Dungloe.

Eamonn Gallagher, 15; Antain Gallagher, 17; Patrick O'Donnell, 44; Kitty O'Donnell, 45; and Peter Leonard, 61.

Of the twenty aboard that night, only one survived – Patrick Gallagher, Eamonn's son. Holding fast to the keel, he stayed alive throughout the night until someone rescued him at nine on Sunday morning. He lost his father, four brothers and two sisters that night in the accident at Béal an Éilín – seven from one house alone!

Nine corpses were recovered on the first day, and between then and Christmas seven more corpses were recovered. Another body was recovered on 15 August 1936 by Charlie Mickey Kitty O'Donnell on Eighter Strand – that of Eamonn Gallagher, the owner of the boat. Seventeen bodies in all were

Patrick Gallagher – the sole survivor of the Arranmore Disaster.
Patrick died on 25 June 1987.

recovered; the two whose bodies were never recovered were Nora Gallagher – Michael's daughter – and Kitty O'Donnell.

Canon John McAteer was our parish priest, and Father Barney Gallagher was the curate on the island. These two priests were a great support to the people in that time; they truly did their very best to console and comfort us all through those days. Canon McAteer died in 1945 and is interred at the side of the church at Acres, Burtonport. Father Gallagher was transferred from the island later; he died when he was parish priest in Gortahork; he's buried up there.

Wednesday 13 November 1935, the day of the funeral, was a day of great sorrow in Arranmore. People came there from everywhere, newsmen, clergy, politicians, as well as all the people of the island. Senator Joseph Connolly, representing the government came down from Dublin; he was up until then the only senator to be a member of the cabinet, he was minister for lands at that time; he also had responsibility for the Gaeltacht areas. It was a short, bitter winter's day, a day that will never be forgotten by anyone who had known what happened at that time.

God rest all those who lost their life; and God grant no district will ever again suffer a disaster the like of that.

RETROSPECT

RETROSPECT

I'm now more than four score years of age, and sitting by the fire I often reflect on the great changes that have come about in my own lifetime. Books and newspapers are to be found in every house today; the situation was completely different when I was growing up. I remember when there were no newspapers sold in any shops around here. There were a few people on the island who used to get a newspaper twice a week through the post – the priest, schoolmasters, and one or two others, and that was it. The men round about would gather in the house of the man who had the paper, and he'd read it aloud to them. I often gave Sheila Beag of Leabgarrow a hand at the housework, and in the afternoon the men of the area would drop in for a chat; as well as that they'd come in to hear Charlie Liam, the man of the house, read the *Derry Journal*. Sheila Beag and her husband had the post office; they also had a bar at that time, and, as I said, she'd send me word when she needed a bit of help. She was kept busy, for she often kept a schoolmaster in her house. A son of Sheila's – we called him Charlie Beag – was a fine fiddler; so what with the reading of the paper, the chat, the storytelling and company of every kind that house was a lively place. You wouldn't find so many there in the summer, however, for they were away working in Scotland at that time of the year, but in winter the house was

Peadar O'Donnell (1893–1986), writer. From 1916 to 1918, he served as headmaster, Leabgarrow School

packed now with the men were back from Scotland.

The writer Peadar O'Donnell, or Peadar Beag as we called him, was one of the teachers who lodged there. He was born and reared in Meenmore near Dungloe, so of course he was just like one of ourselves when he was here. As I recall it now, Charlie Liam seldom read the paper aloud while Peadar was in the house; I think he was shy about doing so when a schoolmaster might be listening. Peadar certainly let the company know what was in the paper, but only now and again would he read it to them. He'd sooner highlight a particular item that would set them disputing and squabbling, for that's when he'd get great delight out of listening to them. During his time here we were never short of news and things to talk about. Peadar came into Arranmore in 1916, the year of the

Rising, and he taught here for the next two years. I can see him still as he was in those days, sitting there in Sheila's house, listening to the company hotly discussing the big events of the day. He was always deeply interested in the problem of migration and, after leaving the island and giving up teaching, he did everything he could to improve the lot of the potato workers in Scotland. He was a great help to them.

But as I keep saying again and again, people's lives today are totally different. We've been getting the Dublin newspapers every day since the 1935 drowning. As well as that, people get English and Scottish newspapers by post, and on top of that there's a great supply of local weekly papers in the shops. There's a radio of some sort in nearly every house, and if you haven't one yourself, you can listen to your neighbour's. Four years ago the electric light came to the island, and I'd say as many as twenty houses have a television now. It's a huge change from our young days. We had nothing like that – our life was just the same as it had been for our ancestors, generation beyond generation, back farther and farther in the past.

So it's no surprise we were captivated by the Búistéir's stories and the songs my mother sang when we were youngsters – there just weren't any other pastimes. A few years before my marriage Doney Green, or Doney Sheáin as we called him, arrived home from Scotland with a thing that amazed us all. It was one of the old style gramophones and the like of it had never been seen before. There was a handle on the side that had to be turned to set the music going, and on the top of it was a horn, a foot and a half in height. The neighbours used to say it was a present from the farmer Doney worked for throughout his life, Robert Love of Ballarno in the Lothians. Doney's son, Séimí, the man I married, told me that that was true indeed:

Love had bought a new gramophone for his family and they had no further use for this one. Anyway, it was a fine Christmas present for Doney – and for the people of the island too; it was looked on as a wonder.

Crowds flocked to the house to listen to the gramophone – the neighbours, people from the middle of the island, people from as far away as Aphort itself. Yes, they'd travel all that distance to hear 'Doney Sheáin's old man'. Doney and his wife Nuala Mór would have a warm welcome for them all, but their house wasn't very big; there were no seats for half the visitors, so they had to make do and sit on the floor. There were only a half dozen records with the gramophone, but that was enough. It was a great novelty for everyone – people were easy pleased in those days. I can't mind the names of those records today, but there's one I do recall, a song with this line – *I am the man that makes the money in the mint*. Lots of the old people round here hadn't much English, so many of them didn't know what sort of a thing a *mint* might be.

The gramophone was played so often that the spring finally broke, and someone was needed to stand at the side of the table and turn the handle to get any sound out of it. One night they were all sitting round listening and one of the neighbours, Dan Liam, was the one turning the handle. With that the 'old man' broke down completely, and Nuala Mór, the woman of the house, was far from pleased – she accused Dan Liam of wrecking the machine, and getting up off her chair, she glared at Dan, and exclaimed: 'Tá Carraig an Duibhleathaigh, tá Carraig Mhic Céachtaigh, Carraig Néill Ruaidh, ach dar mo chonsias, a Dhónaill, gur cheart domh Boilg an Chaca a thabhairt mar leas-ainm ortsa ('There's the Black Weed Rock, there's MacEachtaigh's Rock and there's

Neill Rua's Rock, but, by my soul, the proper title for you, Dan Liam O'Donnell, is the Boilg an Chaca [The Rock of Shit])!' Boilg an Chaca is a rock in Arran Roads near Eighter Island.

Our next-door neighbour was John Boner, Johnny Mór. He was from the mainland, but he came to live on the island after he was married. Our two houses were side by side and we often popped into each other's house throughout our life. They were a pleasant, obliging couple and we treated them as good friends too. Johnny wife's name was Fanny Lyons; however she was Maitiú Lyons's daughter, and was never called anything except Fanny Maitiú. She's dead now these thirty-three years. As I said, she and her husband used to spend evenings in chatting with us and we'd often drop into their house for an evening too. Yes, they really were a lovely couple in their day.

The Búistéir, God be good to him, often told us how Maitiú Lyons first came to the island. He was a native of Glencolumcille and it seems he came one day to sell rough homespun at the fair in Dungloe. At that time he used to go from fair to fair, and he'd set up a small stall along the street. It was sometime around the Great Famine – it was before Charley became landlord of Arranmore – and there was no postal service to the island till he arrived. It's likely that this girl, Nuala Green, had to go out to the fair on some business and she went to buy some of Maitiú's homespun. According to the story they talked about more than his homespun. They took a notion of each other and spent longer talking together than customers usually did. And that was only the start of it, for Nuala went out to the very next fair in Dungloe, and they took up where they left off a month earlier. The bond grew stronger and stronger – from then on there was no parting them. After another fair or two the question of marriage came up. Nuala said she couldn't leave her parents without their consent, but Maitiú was in a hurry over the affair: it would soon be Shrove Tuesday, and he meant to have the matter settled before Lent. As he was leaving the fair in Dungloe, he told Nuala what she was to do in order to let him know how her family felt about it.

'Go home,' said he, 'and talk it over with them. If they're in favour, send me word.'

But now another difficulty cropped up. Neither of them had enough learning to write to the other; in any case there was no letter-post to the island. But that didn't defeat Maitiú.

'If they're happy with the marriage, light a fire on the highest hill near you and I'll be on the look-out for it.'

Nuala did what she was asked to do. On the next fine night she lit the fire to let the man with the homespuns know he was very welcome in Arranmore as a son-in-law. On the hill above Glencolumcille Maitiú was keeping an eye out for the fire; there was now no doubting the message. At the crack of dawn he hurried down to the Rosses and it wasn't the selling of homespuns that was foremost in his mind at this stage. Without delay Nuala Green and himself were married, and after that they made a home for themselves here on the island.

Long ago we often had ghost stories round the fire. I heard the old people talking about the ghost that one of the Boyles encountered about a hundred years ago. This man – Páidín Aoidh Boyle – was living at Gortgar in the middle of the island and Dominick Gallagher, Dominick Beag, was his next-door neighbour in the same townland. The two houses were built there, down below the road, fifty yards apart, no other house between them. The two households were very great with each other; they were always steadfast neighbours; nobody could set them at odds with each other.

A story is told that Páidín Aoidh went out to the hill one day and brought home one of his sheep. He put her in an outhouse for the night and placed a creel and a couple of other things in the doorway to keep her inside. He went off visiting then, but when he returned at bedtime, the creel was no longer in place at the door and the sheep was gone. Páidín reckoned the ewe had gone back to the hill and he'd better go out for her again. It was a bright moonlit night and he thought he'd have no trouble finding her. When he was approaching the Claí na bhFód (the sod ditch between the landlord's land and the tenants' land), coming towards him was a group of men, each of them carrying a creel on his back. There were scraws and bog-parings in every creel as if they were repairing the boundary fence. No wonder Páidín was frightened, and out of fear of them he started to bless himself. Then, finding courage, he was brave enough to address them.

'May I enquire of you if you are men of flesh and blood or are you not?'

One of them answered him as they were moving on about their business in the direction of the Claí na bhFód: 'We are not people of this life at all, but are here serving out our sentence in this manner.'

Back to Dominick Beag and Páidín Aoidh. It seems each of them had a son by the name of Donncha. In their lifetime the two Donncha's – Donncha Dominick and Donncha Páidín – were always great pals; in public they couldn't be parted. And then, what do you think? Donncha Dominick died and the other Donncha was very, very depressed. They had agreed a sort of mutual pact or pledge that if one of them died, he'd come back and see the other one, the one who was alive. But that was only the childish talk of the young and Donncha Páidín had forgotten it totally by this stage.

It was down on Chapel Strand after Donncha Páidín had come ashore from fishing that the other Donncha first appeared to him. He was on his way home, when he realised he had left his pipe behind him in the stern of the boat. There was nothing for it but to go back down again for the pipe. Lifting the pipe he saw the ghost standing in front of him at the bow of the boat. The ghost spoke to him and then he recognised who it was – Donncha Dominick. The ghost wondered that he didn't recognise his old comrade until he spoke to him. Donncha Páidín was seized by fear – as anyone would after an awful shock like that. Donncha Dominick said he'd like them to meet again and he appointed the time and the place where they'd meet the following night. Though he was greatly shaken by what had happened, Donncha managed to make his way home. In the morning he decided to go to the priest and tell him the story.

Father James Hargan was the curate on the island at that time and he was living in Fallagowan a couple of hundred yards along the road east of Páidín Aoidh's house. Donncha told him his story for he wanted to get his advice. When the priest heard about the pledge they had made to each other, he said to Donncha: 'Well, even though you had this pledge, you're not sure if this person was Donncha Dominick, are you?'

The priest then took a piece of sally rod and after he blessed it, he gave it to Donncha and told him what he was to do. Hearing Donncha Páidín Aoidh's story again and again affected me so deeply that the words of the priest still power through my head: 'When you encounter him, bless yourself with this rod and gaze down at his feet, and make sure it is Donncha Dominick who is talking to you. Make sure his feet aren't cloven, for if they are, it is the devil that's there in front of you.'

Donncha Páidín listened to everything the priest said; he thanked him and returned home, but his mind was far from calm as he waited for night to fall when he'd have to go down the road again to meet Donncha Dominick, his friend of many years in this mortal world. Down he would have to go in spite of everything he had been told about the matter.

The other Donncha arrived as he had promised. At that Donncha Páidín took out the sally rod and made the sign of the cross to ward off evil. When the other Donncha saw what he had just done, he seemed somehow disappointed. He spoke, reminding him: 'Ah, it's a pity you didn't recognise me last night. Did you not know we had this pact from long ago?'

Donncha Páidín stumbled out as good an answer as he could manage: 'Well, that pledge hasn't crossed my mind for ages … anyway I believed you'd never be allowed out and about. I haven't much to tell you, but maybe there's something that might be worrying you? Can I can help you in any way?'

And these are the words the other Donncha said in reply: 'I'm well, but there's a small matter still keeping me out of paradise. Tell my family to pay the couple of shillings I owe the tailor, and tell them also to ask the priest to say a mass for my soul and then I'll gain my rest … As for you, keep on living as you are at present and you'll be all right when your day comes. Avoid any backbiting you come across, for there's nothing our Saviour hates more than those people who

264 – Róise Rua

slash and cut each other's character to bits. Always be of good mind, keep on saying your prayers and you'll be in no danger. I cannot tell you much about my existence at present, for I'm not allowed to. Some of the people here are well but, alas, there are more who are not well.'

It's likely the two Donnchas took leave of each other after that; young Donncha Páidín Boyle, deeply affected by what he had just been through, found his way back home; the old people used to say the poor lad never went to mass from then on.

If I were to give an account of all the folklore I heard in my youth, I feel it would fill a whole book. The old people had every kind of folklore and they'd tell us these stories when we were gathered round the fire at night – yarns, superstitions, cures, songs, proverbs and so on. The Búistéir had a particular story he'd often tell about an old woman by the name of Máire; she lived at Gortgar, not far from Páidín Aoidh's house. She was living there long ago in Conyngham the landlord's time, and she was absolutely destitute. Because she had no way of paying the rent, Foster of Roshine – Conyngham's agent – stated that she was to be evicted; it seems he also said that whoever carried out the eviction would be allowed keep her place for themselves. According to the story neighbours arrived one day, threw her out, and then set fire to her wee house. We find it difficult to credit such a story, but I've got no other version than the one the Búistéir told us long ago. Máire had two daughters; one of them had gone to Canada on the free emigration scheme; the other was still living with her mother. Máire had no choice but to take herself off to the poorhouse in Glenties and I believe she died there. It appears that one of her brothers, Phelimy Siút, had gone to Canada a few years before that. Poor Máire composed this lament on how badly she had been treated:

D'éirigh Páidín Aoidh agus labhair sé go caíúil
ag iarriadh orthu éirí agus an t-adhmad a shábháil.
Níor shíl siad a choíche go mbeadh said mar bhí siad
is nach mbeadh fear acu a dhéanfadh dóibh fáras.

Páidín Aoidh rose up and speaking plaintively
advised them bestir themselves and keep an eye on their wood.
They never thought things would turn out as they turned out,
that they'd never have a man who would build them a house.

I Quebec, faraor, atá mo bhunadh uilig 'en tsaol
is ní fheicfidh mé choíche Gráinne.
Dónall Ultach ar a dtús agus Cití, mar a dúirt,
is í Gráinne a chuir cluain ar a cairde.
D'aithris siad i modh rúin domh go raibh Feilimí Siút thar sáile,
I gCeanada ag gearradh a chuid adhmaid.
Tiocfaidh sé go fóill is beidh air iontas rómhór
Fán tsiortáil a tugadh ar Mháire.

All my people, God help me, now live in Quebec;
never again will I set my eyes upon Gráinne.
Daniel Ultach was the first to leave, and then Kitty, who said
it was Gráinne was the one who had hoodwinked her friends.
They told me in confidence Phelimy was away over the sea,
cutting down trees far off in Canada.
One day he'll come back and he will be astonished
At the hardship that was heaped upon Máire.

Not only was the Búistéir great at reciting the legends and stories, he was also a great man to talk for he had a huge store of knowledge, and people often came in for a night's chat. What with the Búistéir's talking and his stories and the songs my mother would sing the night fairly flew in. Even strangers on the island used to drop into the house. A stonemason from Griall in the Annagary district was a frequent visitor; he was working in the island at that time. His name was Phelimy

Sweeney, Phelimy Neddy, and he had a fine voice in his day. He often sang us *Cuach mo Londubh Buí* or *An Chrúbach*. We had another man from Meenmore – Jimmy Boner, or Jimmy Paddy Naois. He was in the island when the pier at Aphort was under construction and he stayed in Johnny Mór's house – he was related to Johnny. He had a good supply of songs, but the only two I remember now are *Neansaí ní Obarlainn* and *Buarach na Bó*.

I remember the winter I came home after the three and a half years I'd worked down in the Lagan. Máire had just returned from Scotland and brought home a little melodeon she had bought in Glasgow. She could play it fairly well, for there were few potato squads long ago that hadn't someone who could play a melodeon, so she already had some practice. Needless to say we spent a lot of our time that winter singing and dancing as well as the knitting. That was the year Niall McCurdy came to the island and he often came in to see us. He was a native of Rathlin Island; he was a stonemason, and he was working at the lighthouse. He had a huge stock of songs between those in English and an even bigger number in Scots Gallic. I wasn't able to learn the words of the Gallic songs very well, but I picked up the airs and I can still lilt them as we sit round the fire.

I'd say there were up to a dozen fiddlers on the island when I was young. We had nothing resembling a dance hall then, but there were plenty of dances going on in kitchens or barns. There was no dancing on the island during the summer, for that's when all the young ones were away at work in Scotland. So the time for the dancing was the winter and spring. The dances didn't cost much. There were times when we were allowed in free, but sometimes there was a small charge – three pence, maybe, or six pence. For those dances there was only one musician, a fiddler or a melodeon player. There was often a raffle too; you were given a ticket when you went in and at the end of the night the tickets were put in a hat; a prize of some sort would go to the person whose number was drawn out – a foal, perhaps, or a calf, maybe even a pair of boots that were too small for their owner!

We also had a thing called a 'fiddler' at that time. A group of men would arrive to do the work for a poor widow or for a man maybe who wasn't fit to do the work himself, and a fiddler was hired for a dance to end the day. If, for instance, the man of the house was ill in the spring and wasn't able to sink a spade in the soil, word was passed around and the men of the area would gather to do the work for him. When the delving or whatever was finished, that night the young ones would come to a house in the neighbourhood and there'd be a dance. Usually there was no admission charge at these 'fiddlers', but if money was collected, it was given to the widow or to the orphans the dance was held in aid of. Sometimes those dances would last till six in the morning, but they were usually over by two or three.

About thirty years ago we had our own pipe band, but it's difficult to keep something like that going in a place like Arranmore. Some of the members left for Scotland or America and it wasn't easy teaching others to take their place. The pipes and the outfits are very expensive – especially in a poor area where there's no steady employment throughout the year.

There was one really great piper in the island in my time. His name was Michael O'Donnell or Mickey Mhicheáil Bhig as he was commonly called. He lived beside the river in the townland of Ballintra, not far from the chapel. There were two of them, himself and his brother, Frank. Tragically, Frank was drowned in Arran Roads when the two of them were on their way out to Burtonport. They were taking a load of potatoes to sell on the mainland. A huge wave broke near them and they were flung overboard. Mickey managed to stay on the surface long enough for a man from Eighter Island to come to their rescue; that fisherman, Charley Tony, managed to save Mickey, but poor Frank was lost. Many people drowned at that same place from the time I reached the age of reason.

As I said already Mickey was an outstanding piper in his day. They say he never used to accept payment for his music. I mind one Sunday long ago when he landed at Pollawaddy and came up the steep road to visit the Búistéir and my mother. It was a fine day in the middle of May and those bound for Scotland were still here in the island. Mickey had his pipes with him that day and he kept playing all the way up from the quay. Everybody in the neighbourhood came to the door to listen to him. Not only that – a crowd of wee children followed him up as far as our house. Step for step they stayed with him up the steep slope except when he had to sit now and again and draw his breath. The Búistéir and my mother gave him the warmest of welcomes. When he had talked to them and had drunk a bowl of tea, he lifted his pipes again, saying: 'It wouldn't be right for me to leave this house without playing a tune for Maighréad and the Búistéir'.

And from then on, right through to nightfall he never stopped. I remember the three of us – Nancy, Máire and myself – were home at the time and we and the young ones of the district went out to dance, and the piper – sitting in the shade – kept on playing. We never did so much dancing as we did that same day, and one of those dances was the *Maggie*

Piggy – a dance we loved doing in those years. I don't have to tell you Mickey and his pipes made it a wonderful afternoon for us all.

Year after year Mickey went to Scotland to work on the farms, and he always took his pipes with him; on the way over and back on the Derry boat he'd play many a tune. And if he had an hour or two to spare and wasn't too tired after his day's work, he'd play at night in the bothy. Many stories were told about him in his years in Scotland. Once he was playing the pipes in the bothy and the women of the district came in to listen to him. Not only was he a great player – there wasn't a tune he didn't know. People were absolutely amazed at his ability to pick up all these tunes. As I said, the women of the farm came into the bothy where he and his workmates were staying. There they were, listening to the piper, and they hadn't the least notion of going home. All the women of the farm were there – the gaffer's wife, the agent's wife, the wives of the cottiers and ploughmen – even the farmer's wife herself. It was getting near tea-time and it seemed to the men in the bothy that it was long past the time these women should be gone back home to their own houses. At last the piper did something that would send them packing. He started to play Irish songs, some that would not be to their liking. He struck up first with *God Save Ireland*, and after that he played *Lá Fhéile Pádraig*. Within moments the trick worked. He'd no sooner played two notes of *Lá Fhéile Pádraig*, than the lot of them upped and hurried off home. You can be sure the same women didn't come back to hear him another night in the bothy!

There was the time too when Mickey was working on a farm close to Edinburgh. One day a piper came to the farmhouse, and when he was told there was another piper – an Irish piper – lodging in the bothy, he came in, pipes and all. He started to talk to Mickey about the pipes and the two of them played together for a while. Then each man played on his own. It seems the piper who came into the bothy was a soldier; he was a piper in the Black Watch, who were stationed in Edinburgh Castle at that time. The upshot of it all was that the two of them were trying to find out who it was knew the most tunes. That was far from easy to establish for both men were really great musicians. It seemed neither had a tune the other didn't know. Then the Arranmore man thought of a tune he reckoned the Scotsman wouldn't be familiar with. He launched into this tune – *Dúlamán na Binne Buí* – and the Scottish piper had to admit he was beaten at last. Mickey Mhicheáil Bhig was the winner; as you'd expect the others in the bothy were delighted. This piper of the O'Donnell clan won great fame in his time, and he richly deserved it. Down the years since then we've never had anyone to equal him.

MY LIFE'S FINAL CHAPTER

In the year after the start of the Second World War Rev. Coslett
Quinn visited me in order to transcribe songs and poems.
He was the first person to come and show an interest in my
folklore. Seán Bán MacGrianna of Rannafast was with him
the first day he called. It was harvest time and I remember I
was busy trying to save the hay and the corn. I sang very many
songs for Rev. Quinn, and he did his best to take down the
words in the verses. The war was going on and the warplanes
often flew overhead on the track of German submarines in
the sea out west from us. It was a fine summer that year, as fine
as we had had for a long time. I remember Seán Bán sitting
on a height outside our house, the sweat pouring off him after
he had walked up the road from the hotel. The Rev. Quinn
also visited Bríd Ward, Biddy Chaithlín, and wrote down her
folklore too. He praised Biddy very highly for the way she
sang the sacred poetry, and he made a point of transcribing
those: *Dán an Toir, Dán na hAoine,* (the Good Friday), *Dan
an Bháis* and others like them. I too had verses from those
songs, but Biddy in her time had them in their entirety. Rev.
Quinn wrote out the words of the poems, but it was a pity he
had no means of capturing the airs that go with them. God
rest poor Biddy; she's dead now these sixteen years; she took
a great deal of her folklore to the grave with her, for no one

bothered to transcribe it apart from the small amount Rev. Coslett Quinn got that year.

I went on singing my collection of songs, and often there was nobody listening except my husband, and maybe he'd be dozing by the fireside in the afternoon. It was eleven years after Rev. Quinn transcribed songs from me before the next person came to me who was interested in my music. It was in 1951 that I met Pádraig Ua Cnáimhsí, or Packie Boner as we knew him in English, a man who was deeply interested in the folklore and the songs I possessed and he did his utmost from then on to write them down and save them for the people who'll come after us. He was from the mainland and at that time he was teaching in Aphort school. He's the man who is now engaged in this story of mine – I'm telling him everything I went through in my life and he's writing it all down. If the pair of us weren't working together, I'd never tell my story. He was the first person who ever advised me to do such a thing and together we've carried out the project.

I remember clearly the very day I first met Packie Boner. As I've said already, I was always friendly with Charley Liam's family in Leabgarrow and I kept up this friendship throughout my life. I have mentioned that I used to help Síle Bhig there at the housework. But the years went by, and in 1951 Síle Bhig and Charley Liam were dead and their children were scattered here and there throughout the world. I've already talked about the time Peadar O'Donnell lodged in the house, but things had changed greatly since then. Two of the family were still at home in Peadar's time, but now they were out in America and Canada, and two others were married and living here in the island. The house and the holding were left to Jack the son, but he now was dead as well and the only ones in the house were his widow Dolly and her family. Packie Boner was married to Sheila, one of her daughters, and as they'd been married only a short time before then, they were still staying in the post office. That's where we first met.

A spring day it was and Dolly Boyle asked me to come and cut seed potatoes for she intended to set a couple of ridges. I told her I'd be happy to do so, and after dinner I went down to Leabgarrow and started on the work. Sometime after three o'clock Packie arrived back from school and when he was eating his dinner, his wife Sheila told him I was out cutting the potatoes in the shed. He said he'd go and see me as soon as he had finished his dinner – and that's how we happened to meet.

There I was, wearing a sack apron, down on my knees, cutting the potatoes as fast as I could, when out he came, and me anxious to head for home as soon as I'd finished the job. There was a pile of split potatoes in front of me on the floor and the discarded pieces to the side out of the way. Packie bid me good day and we chatted away in the natural manner country people do. He wanted to get to know about the songs I knew, and because of that I had to sing him one or two songs. I'm not very sure now what songs they were, but among them, I think, were *Mall Dubh an Ghleanna (The Black Spot in the Glen)* and *An Bonnán Buí (The Yellow Bittern)*. He looked really pleased listening to me. He said goodbye, but promised he'd come up to my house and write down the words of some of the songs. That's how the link between us started, a friendship that has continued ever since, and that's how it happened he went on to write this story here. He's always done everything he could for me, and if weren't for him, it's certain no notice would ever be taken of me or my songs.

He wrote down about seventy of the songs I had and I'd often sing them on his visits to the house. He wrote to the Folklore Commission in Dublin about me, and they sent Seán Ó hEochaidh to make a tape-recording of my songs. After that word about me was passed on to Radio Éireann, and they sent Proinsias Ó Conluain to put me on the radio. I was on the radio for the first time in 1952, and since then I've been on the radio many a time. Séamas Ennis and a man from the BBC arrived one day to record more songs. It's grand that music like that can now be heard on the radio; what a pity there was nothing like that when my mother and the Búistéir and Biddy Chaithlín were alive; there was a whole lot of others like them and they carried their wealth to the grave.

'We'll be singing all the time in Heaven', my mother used to say long ago, humming a song as she went about the housework. We always had a great love of music and it was a great blessing in our time; it lifted the sadness from us; sure, that in itself was a great thing.

But now, at the age we've arrived at, we're drawing close to the end of our life and the end of our days. The bloom has gone off anyone who has left four score years behind him, and you can't expect the best of health after that. In our time we worked very hard to keep ourselves alive, and the signs of it are there today – we're worn out and we're shaky too and we're often far from healthy. Trying to survive is difficult enough for old people anywhere in the country, but I believe it's a hundred times worse for those who live on an island. They're afraid they'll be struck down by a sudden illness and will have to go off out to the hospital, perhaps at some untimely hour of the night. They're afraid too that they might run out of turf and be left without a fire. We dread the winter, but we welcome the spring and the arrival of the cuckoo. The cuckoo's song encourages us and gives our hearts a lift for another while. It's hard for old people to move out and about in the darkness of winter, but they take heart as soon as 'March with its red shins' has gone. That's the way it is with us now; we only look ahead from one day to the next, and we give thanks to God for the health we're given each day. Long ago the Búistéir would go on and on about the loss of health and the afflictions of old age. But my mother was a woman who had little sympathy for him on that score. She'd say to him: 'Too bad about ye! It's content and grateful you ought to be after the long life God has given you; it'd fit you better at this stage to be gettin' ready for your journey home.'

The pair of them – the Búistéir and my mother – each had a long life. The Búistéir was just one year short of the hundred when he died in 1926, and six years before him – when she was eighty-six – God called my mother.

And now we too are at the same stage. We're getting ready for home. We're prepared just like people about to start a journey – our bags have been packed for many a day, and here we are waiting the call any day now. We have finished our toiling and our ploughing through the sea of this life, and nobody can begrudge us the comfort and the peace we've won at last in old age. My sister, Máire and I often played wee houses long ago here and there up at the Búistéir's. In the evening as the sun was going down behind us in the west, it would light up the windows of the houses on the mainland. As we gazed at those houses, lots of the windows looked as if they were made of gold. Often Máire would stand at the gable staring at the houses out there, and she'd say to me: 'Nach deas iad. Nár dheas a bheith amuigh ag na tithe sin a bhfuil na fuinneoga óir iontu? (Aren't they lovely? Wouldn't it be wonderful to be out at those houses with their windows of gold?)'

But then the sun would set and that put an end to all the things we had seen. Those windows of gold were only the fancies of children. The golden windows lasted only a short while every day, and there were days when there wasn't the least sign of them. Often here sitting by the fire at evening thoughts along those lines come into my mind. You could say I spent a good part of my life pursuing windows of gold – in Iniskerragh, Tyrone, Scotland – but in the heel of the hunt they deceived us. That's the way it is with people in this life.

Here we are now, the two of us sitting at the fireside with our toes in the ashes, as the old people used to say. The race of this life and its stresses are as now good as over in our case and we have earned our rest at long last. We're people who always did the best we could, and I'd say God won't be sore on us. Our life is a wee bit lonely these years, for many of those we grew up with aren't living nearby any more; a great many of them, alas, are dead, and those that are still alive have sunk their roots elsewhere, in Scotland, in America or other parts the world. Today we're just like Oisín after the Fianna long ago. It can't be helped. God's will be done. The Fianna have all gone ahead of us, and we, like Oisín, have to follow on behind them.

When we're reciting the rosary by the fire at night, we still say one of my mother's prayers to mark the end of our day's work. It's a fitting prayer for the end of our lives too, for after all what is a person's life but days and years each one of them following the one that went before? My mother had no books or anything else of the sort; even so, she taught us our prayers

277 - Róise Rua

round the fire as soon as we were fit to recite them after her. Therefore, in honour of my mother, and in honour of the Mother of God, I feel there's no better way to complete this story of my life than by reciting here that prayer my mother used to say long ago:

A Mhaighdean Mhuire, a Mháthair Dé,
A bhfuil tiarnas na cruinne go huile ár do láimh go léir,
Faigh impí ó d'Aon Mhac a d'fhulaing an Pháis go géar,
Gach gábh a mbeimid ann tar agus tarrtháil sinn.

Aiméan.

Blessed Virgin Mary, Mother of God,
Who holds in His hands the lordship of all creation,
Implore God's Only Son who suffered the cruel Passion
To come and free us from every danger we find ourselves in.

Amen.

Róise Rua at the end of her life. Antain McGowan, the renowned County Donegal architect, took this photo of Róise two years before her death.

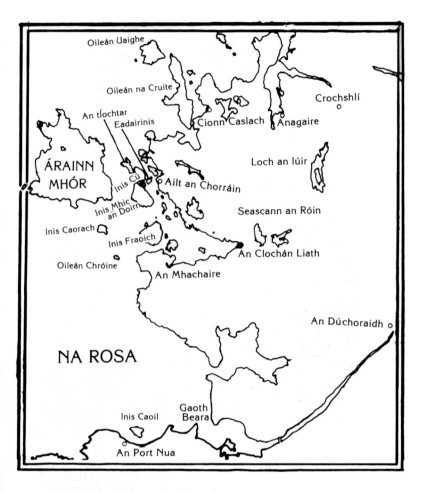

From the top

Oileán Uaighe – Owey Island; Oileán na Cruite – Cruit Island; Cionn Caslach – Kincasslagh; Crochshlí – Crolly; Anagaire – Annagary; An tÍochtar – Eighter; Eadarinis – eder/idirinish; Inis Cú – Inishcu; Loch an Iúir – Lough Anure; Ailt an Chorráin – Burtonport; Inis Mhic an Doirn – Rutland Island; Seascann an Róin – Sheskinarone; Inis Caorach – Iniskerragh; Inis Fraoich – Inishfree Upper; Oileán Chróine – Illancrone; An Clochán Liath – Dungloe; An Mhachaire – Maghery; An Dúchoraidh – Doochary; Gaoth Beara – Gweebarra river, estuary, bay; Inis Caoil – Inishkeel; An Port Nua – Portnoo.

APPENDIX

Pádraig Ua Cnáimhsí was born in the townland of Cruickamore two miles from Burtonport, the Rosses, County Donegal in March 1918. He attended St Enda's College in Dublin and then studied in St Patrick's Training College in Drumcondra, Dublin where he qualified as a primary schoolteacher in 1938.

He taught in Arranmore Island for forty-one years and retired in 1983.

Packie had always been deeply interested in Irish, history, folklore and music; on meeting Róise Rua, he instantly realised how important her story was, and zealously set about writing it down. He was already well versed in the history and folklore of the island and that served him well when he commenced this work. He died on 14 November 2007. Ar lámh dhéis Dé go raibh a anam.

Proinsias Ó Conluain wrote the foreword to the original *Róise Rua*. He had visited Róise Rua and recorded her songs for Radio Éireann in the 1950s with Seán Ó hEochaidh, the well known folklore collector from Teelin, County Donegal. Seán also wrote *Rothaí Mór an tSaoil* a book about the life of Gort a' Choirce man Mící MacGabhann and his adventures in Ireland and in the gold mines of the Yukon. Seán died 18 January 2002. Proinsias Ó Conluain is retired and living in

Dublin. He is widely credited, though his work with Radio Éireann in the 1950s, with being one of the people who ensured that Irish music remained sufficiently prominent in the national consciousness until better days came for the music when it enjoyed a strong revival in the 1960s. *Tá ar mbuíochas tuillte aige.*

Niall Ó Donaill who was from Loch an Iuir, County Donegal proof read the original *Róise Rua* book. He was an authority on Donegal Irish. He published an Irish dictionary and wrote many books and articles including a history of his native Rosses, *Na Glunta Rosannacha* (*The Generations of the Rosses*). Niall died on 13 October 1995. *Suaimhneas síoraí tabhair dó a Thiarna.*

Rev. Coslett Quinn first met Róise with Seán Bán MacGrianna, of Rann a' Fheirde in the late 1940s when he took an interest in her songs. He was a Church of Ireland clergyman, a lecturer and an Irish language enthusiast all his life. He knew a fair bit about translation himself as he had translated the Bible, the New Testament to *An Tiomna Nua ár dTiarna.* He also translated Brian Merriman's 'Cúirt an Mheán Oiche' to English as *The Midnight Court.* He wrote much material in Irish including *Sceálta Inis Eogháin* a book on the folklore of that area. He wrote to Packie Boner in Irish from Belfast after *Róise Rua* was published. He told of how to his amusement he was in Waterstones Bookshop in 8 Royal Avenue (Belfast) and came across *Róise Rua* for sale. He talked of Róise, Arranmore, Gola Island, the poets of the Fews, Dáll MacCuarta and Art MacChumhaidh, his own father he said like his friend Thomas Ó Fiaich had been from the Fews, County Armagh – and he spoke of times past and present. He died in 1995. *Go ndéana Dia trocaire ar a anam uasal.*

About two years or less ago I was collecting money for a charity I was involved in called Charity Aids Partnership Africa. I spoke on Foyle Radio about the charity and the work it was doing to alleviate the suffering caused by the Aids epidemic in Africa. Arising from that radio interview J.J. Keaveny asked me to come and visit him, which I did. J.J made a very generous contribution to the charity referred to. I found J.J. to be an attractive person and we became close friends. Although he was bedridden he was good humoured, mentally alert and good company. When he told me that he was working on translating *Róise Rua* I agreed to help him to get the book published. After Packie Boner died in November 2007, I became involved with Packie's sons Dermot and Seán who also assisted J.J. in getting a draft of the book finished. This was largely achieved by June 2008. J.J.'s health deteriorated in the summer of 2008 and he was unable to finish the draft for publication. He died on 17 September 2008. *Go ndéana mhaith air.*

Bart O'Donnell, Derry City, 2009

INDEX

A

Aberdeen 150
Achill 99, 106, 108, 112, 245
Acres 26, 68, 85, 213, 234, 251
Ailsa Craig 109, 113, 206
America 21, 28, 30, 48, 49, 74, 115,
    157, 172, 173, 177, 182, 197,
    231, 232, 267, 272, 276
Annagary 12, 69, 122, 129, 141,
    179, 180, 229, 265
Aphort 20, 36, 48, 73, 135, 142,
    152, 177, 217, 220, 222, 236,
    246, 247, 248, 258, 266, 272
Ardara 72, 223
Ardrossan 106, 113
Arran Head 177
Arranmore 10, 16, 19, 21, 25, 27,
    29, 32, 33, 34, 39, 42, 43, 44,
    48, 49, 53, 56, 57, 58, 59, 61,
    62, 63, 68, 70, 71, 73, 81, 83,
    85, 92, 99, 102, 104, 106, 129,
    130, 132, 134, 137, 139, 141,
    148, 155, 158, 159, 162, 167,
    170, 171, 173, 176, 177, 179,
    181, 182, 183, 184, 185, 189,
    190, 195, 197, 198, 202, 204,
    205, 207, 209, 210, 211, 212,
    214, 217, 218, 220, 221, 224,
    225, 226, 228, 231, 233, 234,
    235, 236, 238, 241, 242, 243,
    245, 246, 247, 248, 249, 250,
    251, 256, 259, 260, 267, 270,
    280, 281
Arran Roads 25, 27, 87, 103, 104,
    147, 172, 197, 198, 219, 230,
    231, 241, 248, 259, 268
Artigarvan 76
Ayrshire 102, 107, 109, 113, 114,
    231

B

Ballard 91
Ballarno 150, 170, 257
Ballina 104
Ballinacarrick 31, 32
Ballinamore 189, 194, 195
Ballintra 27, 91, 137, 143, 177,
    184, 226, 267
Ballybofey 68, 69, 70, 71, 229, 230
Ballymagorry 124
Ballymanus 13, 180
Ballyness Bay 104, 227
Béal an Éilín 234, 249, 250
Bearney 58
Belcruit 27, 243
Belfast 175, 179, 241
Belmullet 99
Bloody Foreland 38, 171
Boylagh Bay 53, 56, 174, 176
Braade 141
Brockagh 80, 216
Broomielaw 105
Bunbeg 80, 224
Burtonport 10, 19, 33, 34, 58, 65,
    66, 67, 68, 70, 81, 83, 85, 86, 93,
    138, 152, 180, 185, 200, 205,
    207, 214, 217, 218, 222, 223,
    224, 226, 227, 228, 229, 230,
    231, 232, 233, 234, 236, 237,
    239, 246, 247, 251, 268, 280

C

Calf Island 103, 104, 121, 198,
    235, 239
Calhame 129
Canada 173, 176, 177, 197, 201,
    264, 265, 272
Carbad 71
Cardiff 239

Carrickvickeaghty 27
Cashelnageeragh 138
Castlederg 125, 126, 127
Cloghcor 27, 29, 75, 78, 137
Clogherdillure 67, 152
Cloghwally 31, 220
Cloughaneely 104, 127, 129
Clyde 105, 122
Creeslough 144, 233, 234
Crolly 220
Cruickamore 70, 280
Cruit Island 27, 146, 173, 220
Cupar 116

D

Derry 9, 10, 12, 65, 78, 80, 93, 101,
    113, 118, 119, 120, 121, 122,
    124, 159, 172, 178, 179, 218,
    227, 229, 230, 231, 237, 246,
    247, 255, 269
Derrydruel 31
Derryloaghan 31
Diarach 141
Donemana 73
Doochary 31, 69, 71
Doon Well 66, 230
Down 185, 197, 200, 228
Downings 104
Dreen 132, 143, 222
Dublin 11, 39, 44, 54, 101, 132,
    179, 215, 223, 233, 251, 257,
    274, 280, 281
Duhoma 99
Dumbartonshire 102, 119
Dungloe 25, 29, 30, 31, 47, 54, 66,
    67, 68, 70, 80, 160, 161, 172,
    200, 203, 204, 206, 213, 216,
    220, 224, 225, 226, 228, 229,
    231, 242, 250, 256, 259, 260

E

Edinburgh 114, 116, 118, 149,
    150, 154, 155, 159, 172, 269,
    270

Eighter 197, 198, 224, 240, 250,
    268
Elly Bay. 238
England 47, 99, 152, 169, 171,
    173, 197, 208
Errigal 13, 38
Erris 173, 182

F

Falcarragh 233
Fallagowan 49, 137, 138, 142, 207,
    211, 213, 262
Fanad 46, 142
Fifeshire 100, 102, 113
Fintown 70, 227
Fraserburgh 150

G

Galashiels 106
Galway 10, 11, 64, 174
Gartan 47
Girvan 106, 107, 110, 116, 206
Glasgow 101, 104, 105, 110, 113,
    116, 118, 120, 122, 159, 173,
    175, 179, 182, 218, 227, 230,
    245, 246, 266
Glencolumcille 259, 260
Glendennon 80
Glenfinn 71, 189
Glen Head 103, 171
Glenmornan 9, 73, 75, 76, 78
Glenties 30, 31, 32, 72, 83, 84, 85,
    86, 89, 98, 117, 119, 128, 130,
    142, 147, 175, 177, 200, 213,
    226, 264
Gortgar 40, 216, 260, 264
Gortin 73
Gortnasade 104, 217
Greenock 105, 119, 120, 122, 124
Grianlach 78, 80
Gweebarra Bay 31, 61, 220, 224
Gweebarra River 31
Gweedore 12, 104, 127, 131, 147,
    173, 179, 214, 219, 224, 242

Gweesala 99

H

Hebrides 148
Helensburgh 119

I

Illancrone 59
Illion 52, 53, 59, 64, 210
Inisbofin 182, 183
Inishcoo 204
Inishfree 52, 58, 224
Inishfree Upper 52
Inish Gé 238
Inishowen 80, 124
Inish Saille 224
Iniskerragh 36, 44, 53, 54, 55, 56,
    57, 58, 59, 62, 63, 64, 85, 86,
    102, 174, 201, 202, 203, 204,
    217, 223, 224, 276

K

Keadew 29
Kelso 106
Kilmarnock 106, 116
Kincasslagh 104, 179, 204, 217,
    218, 219, 279
Kintyre 105, 113, 123, 127
Kirkintilloch 112, 245

L

Lagan 20, 38, 41, 46, 49, 53, 64, 66,
    67, 73, 80, 81, 82, 88, 98, 103,
    114, 119, 125, 127, 149, 157,
    206, 230, 266
Lanarkshire 102, 113
Largs 110
Larne 179
Leabgarrow 36, 37, 40, 44, 45, 49,
    64, 66, 130, 131, 132, 137, 139,
    143, 145, 152, 184, 190, 205,
    211, 213, 233, 240, 241, 243,
    255, 256, 272, 273
Leabrannagh 76
Letterkenny 34, 65, 128, 172, 229,
    230, 233, 234
Lettermacaward 84, 85
Lifford 76, 206, 209, 211, 212, 213
Liverpool 239
Lothians 102, 106, 113, 148, 257
Lough Foyle 13, 124
Lough Meela 200
Lough Swilly 11, 80, 81, 229, 233

M

Magheragallen 173
Magheraroarty 217
Maghery 137
Maidens 113
Malin 173, 182
Manorcunningham 80
Marameelan 217
Mayo 99, 100, 102, 106, 108, 148,
    219, 238, 245
Meath 207
Meenanalbany 200, 212
Meendrain 54
Meenmore 28, 29, 34, 256, 266
Milltown 76, 78
Mountcharles 223
Moville 10, 13
Moyle, Sea of 124
Muckish 38
Mull of Kintyre 105, 109, 113, 127
Murlog 73

N

Newry 139
Newtowncunningham 80
Norway 170, 235, 237, 238

O

Omagh 73
Orkneys 148
Owencarrow 233

Owey 224

P

Perthshire 102, 106, 113
Peterhead 150
Ploghogue 47, 62, 70, 86, 142
Pollawaddy 64, 103, 138, 182, 198,
    208, 210, 211, 213, 220, 235,
    236, 237, 238, 268
Portaferry 197, 200
Portpatrick 110

Q

Queensferry 100

R

Rannafast 12, 224, 271
Raphoe 223
Renfrewshire 113
Rinnanean 55, 62, 102, 142
Roninis 56, 58, 61, 174
Rosguill 104
Roshine 138, 204, 207, 223, 228,
    264
Rosses 25, 28, 29, 30, 42, 58, 67,
    70, 72, 73, 80, 82, 83, 84, 94,
    104, 115, 127, 137, 138, 159,
    169, 173, 175, 207, 210, 215,
    217, 218, 219, 220, 223, 224,
    229, 242, 260, 280, 281
Rutland Harbour 42, 58, 137, 198,
    199, 217, 218, 224, 235, 237

S

Sceardán 71
Scotland 9, 16, 20, 41, 47, 49, 58,
    61, 74, 81, 88, 89, 96, 97, 98, 99,
    101, 102, 103, 105, 107, 108,
    113, 114, 115, 116, 118, 119,
    120, 122, 124, 127, 130, 148,
    149, 150, 152, 155, 157, 159,
    162, 164, 165, 166, 167, 168,
    169, 170, 171, 172, 175, 178,
    179, 201, 206, 210, 215, 217,
    219, 227, 230, 231, 245, 246,
    249, 255, 256, 257, 266, 267,
    268, 269, 276
Scraigathoke 45
Screig an tSeabhaic 20, 74, 141,
    220
Shallogans 31
Sheskinarone 25, 26, 28, 29, 79,
    223, 279
Sion Mills 73
Sionnach Point 199, 200
Sky, Isle of 148
Slane 207
Sliabh Sneachta 38
Sligo 120, 182, 197, 241
Spike 210, 211, 212
Spike Island 210, 211
Strabane 9, 66, 71, 72, 75, 76, 78,
    119, 122, 124, 125, 127
Stranorlar 71, 229

T

Teelin 20, 280
Templecrone 173, 199, 200, 242
Termon 56, 204, 233
Tory Island 38, 104, 171, 173, 180,
    182, 241
Tourmakeady 99
Traighenagh 58, 217, 224, 226
Trá Ishkirt 33
Tyrone 9, 64, 67, 76, 78, 80, 125,
    127, 149, 157, 206, 276
Tyrone. 9, 64, 78, 125, 149, 157

W

Westport 103, 104, 106, 120, 121,
    219, 245
White Inch 105
Wigtown 106
Wigtownshire 102

ALSO FROM MERCIER PRESS

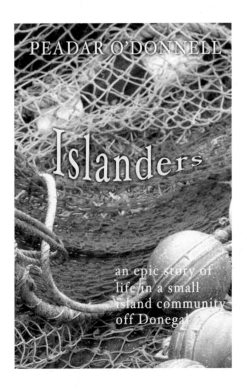

ISLANDERS
PEADAR O'DONNELL

ISBN: 978 1 85635 472 1

Islanders is an epic story of life in a small island community of Donegal, written by one of Ireland's greatest historical and literary figures, Peadar O'Donnell.